SYDNEY JOURNALS

Reflections 1970–2000

Antigone Kefala

Published by Transit Books
1250 Addison St #103, Berkeley, CA 94702
www.transitbooks.org

ISBN: 979-8-893380-25-5 (paperback)
Cover design by Sarah Schulte | Typesetting by Transit Books
Printed in the United States of America

9 8 7 6 5 4 3 2 1

PRAISE FOR ANTIGONE KEFALA

"Marvelous . . . The product of a mind that is as self-sufficient as it is self-assured."

JACOB BROGAN, *THE WASHINGTON POST*

"Moving reflections on the tension between modern life and the life of the mind . . . [*Sydney Journals*] never fails to render itself in full color, at perfect pitch."

PUBLISHERS WEEKLY, STARRED REVIEW

"The pleasure of *The Island* is in its layered sentences, which ask to be unraveled and savored. Like an abstract painting, the book is an atmosphere, a universe with its own rules."

MEARA SHARMA, *THE BELIEVER*

"In poetry as in prose, Antigone Kefala has made the fragment her form. It's a form that embodies both salvage and destruction. [*Late Journals*] bears moving witness to a distinctive, cosmopolitan vision and an unwavering faith in the power and integrity of art."

MICHELLE DE KRETSER,
AUTHOR OF *THEORY & PRACTICE*

"*Sydney Journals* (2008) and *Late Journals* (2022) showcase Kefala's distinctive, cosmopolitan vision . . . There is wonderful generosity in Kefala's acknowledgment of the creative work that matters to her, and a sense of celebration in her intransigent faith in the value and power of art."

JUDGES' CITATION,
PATRICK WHITE LITERARY AWARD

BY ANTIGONE KEFALA

PUBLISHED BY TRANSIT BOOKS

The Island

CONTENTS

SYDNEY JOURNALS

JOURNAL I

JANUARY

Very, very hot. The city humid and alive with people. Reading Montale, his critical writing. Very good, ironic, but seldom enthusiastic, his inner self is constantly waiting for something to overwhelm him, but nothing happens, his sense of irony, and of knowing more than the thing observed, slightly undermines the moment. Harsh on Brancusi.

All religions, romantic notions related to the Absolute—how to reach it, touch it, draw strength from it. Such a force, I imagine, would burn us out—if touched.

Jane Austen in a letter to Fanny: "Single women have a dreadful propensity for being poor."

Yesterday a heatwave, the night oppressively hot, no wind, just this stale air coming through the windows. Fell asleep.

Toward morning the wind came up, blowing in short gusts, ruffling the bedclothes, as if human. Above it the sound in me of a didgeridoo playing, a low continuous hum and then these explosions of sound, at a higher pitch, cries of birds, shimmers of light on the water.

Little is visible on his face, yet they say he is dying. Friends come for lunch. We admire the view over the hills, the garden where the passionfruit flowers are out. The most exotic of forms, with two rings of petals, the lower one blue, the upper a series of sculptured hieroglyphics. The trees are growing, the cats lie in the shade, far away the blue ocean.

Vulnerability—he returns again and again to stories about the past, when he was small and his father would take him to the pictures, going back to a safe period.

This fate that is waiting silently inside us to unfold . . .

FEBRUARY

Ruark rang. He had been in bed with a cold. He came out of the house yesterday, for the first time in days, still feverish. He was looking at Sydney, he had been reading Freud on myths and totemism. The traffic stopped at some point, he was looking down a narrow lane, through to another, somehow the accumulation of signs, houses, the density of it all, he felt that Sydney had now the weight to create a culture. If one were to put all the forces on a grid he said, maybe we would reach what the French call—*pesanteur.*

I was telling him that when we first came out of Europe and for many years, we suffered physically from this lack of historical weight. Something that totally unbalanced us, an element that was lacking in the air, in the water, in the streets, in life, some substance that had become part of our ongoing, elemental necessity.

Ved Mehta's depressing story on TV about his Oxford University friends—committing suicide, killing their fathers with axes, all these boys' clubs in which they sing with one voice, drink as one and have the same brutal attitudes to women. Philosophers? What sort of inner equipment is this?

I went to the cemetery yesterday. The place milky-white and empty, the sea far away. A strong wind was blowing, the same sense of desolation about the place, slightly more resistant to it now after so many years.

Over dinner, the young were laughing a great deal. It was good to hear this energy coming out, these high spirits related to nothing but youth.

"I should like to float out of life," Joan said to me. But life had its own ideas and in the meantime she could no longer live alone in the house. We were all there to help with the move. She looked at us as if a fallen queen trying to maintain her dignity among all these assassins that had come to destroy her life. They had already taken the piano away. She looked very thin and somehow disconnected from the scene. She suddenly asked in a naive, detached voice: "What am I going to do?"

MARCH

The days very still and very hot. The light dusted over the city. No one called, no one came. Very pleased with the silence. At night dreamt that I was in a Greek square, wide, made of marble, totally empty. Entries from four points, as if the setting of a game. At one end large flowers, trees, made of transparent material in angel pink-apricot, Mother's colors. They were moving in the wind, immense petals, beautifully transparent and delicate . . .

The restaurant austere looking but the food quite good. Everyone discussing work, new positions, possibilities. Yet it seemed that none of them had heard someone with a different accent for some time. They were listening to me politely, with an increased amount of attention, as if I were an invalid, so that the air became charged while I spoke. I found it difficult to deal with that amount of artificial attention, attacked by it, so that I lost my way, had these long pauses looking for the most ordinary expressions.

APRIL

The autumn cry of birds in the air above the park, the milky transparency of the air above the trees, diffused in the morning sunlight. A resonance now far away, now near, urgent, repetitive.

In the morning, in the tree, a bird with a voice of sandpaper went on and on rubbing at it gutturally. Then a chorus of other birds would come in at intervals. A storyteller?

Family meeting? Some important message being imparted. All quiet now.

In a biography of Giacometti: "He felt that in this world there can be no final view of things. Disavowing all possibilities he undertook each work as a fresh assault on the impossible."

At the old wharf for the performance. Sydney looking very beautiful at night, lighted up with the moon on top of the buildings, colored reflections on the water, the sea, between the two sides, a lake. An intimate feeling that you could have touched the other side if you stretched your hand.

Kate came for afternoon tea. Her house full of young people, their skins alive, glowing with youth and health. Looking at them she feels that she is one of them, but when she goes to the bathroom and looks into the mirror, it is her mother's face that looks back—displeased. We laughed.

We drove out to the farm. The countryside full of green rolling hills, constantly inviting you to reach the next one, see what is behind it.

At night we lit a fire in the open and talked. The moon was up, a beautiful full moon, a transparent luminosity was falling over the hills, the trees, as if filtered from some unseen source.

Then the horses approached, wanting company too. Powerful animals, in the light of the fire they appeared massive, mythical beings, the white one especially, the light falling on the planes of his head made of marble. But his eyes, very human, soft and humid looking at us.

Late at night, the moon round and very large, low on the horizon, in the absolute silence. Around us rusty objects, horse trailers, stables that were falling down, parts of cars and the old homestead, abandoned now.

Gilbert Becaud—an interesting documentary on the French singer. He was analysing the essence of his style on stage, a style which everyone had predicted will demolish him as a singer. He said: "La peur me déclenche . . ."

We can all say with him—fear triggers us, launches us, releases us . . .

MAY

At the exhibition last night. A young crowd all dressed in black. The paintings looked good on the white walls, the high factory ceiling. The young painter was there, the thin, wiry Greek, laughing quite freely and talking about his gardening. This is how he makes his living—compost-making; the combustion of grass—sometimes, at night, he puts the outside lights on to see the transparent blue smoke rising out of the heap.

I asked for some news on the aesthetic front, but they were not forthcoming.

Driving through the National Park after the fires, the green already coming up from the ground covering the black tree trunks . . . nature and the desire to live.

We stopped to photograph these beautiful black trees, the charred candle-like flowers sitting on the branches as if black birds, some dark song about the underworld, stark against the blue sky.

Writing about Rodin, Rilke once observed that "Fame is only the summation of all the misunderstandings accumulating around a new name."

Trying to write, one needs so much confidence in oneself to carry even a sentence. The moment the level goes down one realizes the futility of all things, the thin nature of the enterprise and language that refuses to work.

Looking at all this violence everywhere, in life, in films, we are constantly forgetting how vulnerable we are . . . no one seems to remember how very vulnerable we are.

After the opening we walked over Pyrmont Bridge, walked into this golden light over the sea. The city, an artificial kingdom made of glass, lights.

J. was saying that she is trying to live as much as possible in the present, but I said, writing is constantly about the past, one does nothing but rake it, like sand in a Japanese garden.

At Abdul's for dinner. The place cold and empty, a dark night, the whole area which before used to teem with people, now as if abandoned, the food slightly tired.

We ate quickly, talked of M.'s death, this amazing instinct for self-destruction that the whole family had. His early reviews that we used to read with Mother, an amazing mixture of erudition, sensitivity and intellectual flamboyance—so rare.

His death such a waste. The last time I had met him at a launch in a pub at the Rocks, his second pair of eyes was emerging diffidently from behind his glasses, vulnerable and shy. The fast flowing of his voice, a jagged tempo, the uncertain, slightly awkward movements of his thin limbs, his walk, swimming through the air. A vestige of a youthful, authoritative tone in his voice, the one that he used in his reviews. I was talking to him about it—"something not acceptable any longer," he said, "could not be repeated."

This amazing idea in all of us that we are indestructible, that the body will take everything and deal with it, again and again.

JUNE

In Melbourne for the conference, went to visit Joan to see how she is getting on.

She was downstairs in the flat complaining bitterly about the cold, repeating herself, unfocused, the family trying to cope as best they could.

At the table she put on her usual airs of a fallen royalty that had known better times, carrying her unplaced meaning above the young heads at the table, listening, frightened at the spectacle and less capable of taking it than we were, the older ones, hardened now, taking in this transformation with more equanimity, waiting for our turn, what form will it take, will we too drift in and out of memory, speak of details of little interest to anyone but ourselves . . .

Around the table they were eating in a strained silence, with white faces, tight lips, the dining room cold, the house, which in her imagination had always appeared grand and imposing, now shrunk with time.

Over coffee in the drawing room she confessed to me about this inner chill she now seemed to carry permanently since

Stefan's death. She said in this young, naive voice: "I thought we were going to live in our house forever . . ."

In the dining room of the old hotel having breakfast. Georgia's voice high on her continuous excitement, telling stories.

The decor in dark red discolored with time, smoky mirrors, Vietnamese waiters, Australian food of the early period—tinned fruit, elderly sausages, overcooked gluey eggs. A historical food that was still being preserved to be offered to the genuine connoisseurs. They were sitting at the tables pretending to be discussing sotto voce, but in fact noticing, disapprovingly, all these foreigners and the noise they were making.

Zoë was talking about her mother, the recent divorce and her inability to deal with it, even though she had always wanted to be free, as if the means to reach that freedom had been taken away from her.

The readings at the conference: On stage Yota's face looked sad, but the poem about her mother's life was very good. Somber, spare, bitter, she had found the exact language.

Tess was frowning, concentrating, then she read these lively dialogues, brides newly arrived in the country, discussing their older husbands' performances, then the powerful birth scene. An amazing mixture of Greekness and Australian small country town lives. Her voices and her tempo totally one with the text.

Everyone constantly going for oversimplification, things evident, intellectually hard, what they don't seem to grasp is that climates develop certain types of intellectuality, that the intellect is dependent on sensibility, that you are not dealing with a universal neutral instrument that can carry the same nuances everywhere, that understanding is related to local conditions, a past, history, a way of life.

This current illusion of the universality of everything, induced one assumes by the new technologies . . .

Nina's letter with the photographs brought back the image of Aunt Marilla, living in that old wooden house, her gestures shaped by her early life still carrying social manners, an implied elegance, intellectual concerns, alertness to the world, thoughtfulness, while around her the house was slowly disintegrating, the floorboards full of holes . . .

Then the daughter, the breakdown, the hospital rape, the child. The past seldom discussed, the war, the total destruction.

Last night I dreamt that I was in the National Gallery, the snakes were coming out of the Aboriginal paintings, moving, alive. They brought a guard to watch over them so that the visitors would not be scared.

JULY

At the opening of the new exhibition, last night.

When we arrived the place electrified with the colors of the paintings and vodka with cranberry juice.

Naive, fairytales, magic birds, but slightly too glossy. The gallery full of people, everyone talking to everyone, intimate stories it seemed . . . this man talking to himself, to me, thin, a European-looking man, as if the formation of these years in another landscape is still clinging to us after all this time, coming out of our faces, the position of our bodies.

He had the thin face of Celan in the late photos, with a similar expression in his eyes, sad, uncertain.

What are these constant fields between us in which the ground bristles with misplaced understandings . . .

The apricot tree already in bloom. Yesterday, late afternoon, hanging the washing, looked up, the delicate flowers were already out, transparent wings in the cold sunlight, a gauze light passing through them, the transparency of a sticky fluid coming out of a cocoon.

July, the month of death anniversaries.

Dream last night. I was in a room where someone was dying. Chairs all around the walls, as in a Greek setting, the room in semi-darkness, murmur of voices, people waiting on the chairs. The dying high on a dais, small somehow.

I was speaking to the dying man. The woman had apparently died already. Only the eyes of the man were visible. He wanted to see water. Above the dais, suspended in the air, was a tap. I turned it on, the water came down, an illusion of water, diffused through some source of light from above, the water sparkling. The eyes of the man were pleased, he made a sign that it was enough and I turned the tap off. As I looked at him, his eyes began to fade slowly under his eyelids, a slow movement, the eyes very black and then they went out—gently.

I thought, this is how it is, pressed my face to the cover of the book in which the eyes seemed to be embedded, as if the body of the person, the surface smooth and iced, the book was already beginning to disintegrate.

I thought—death had come—and began to cry . . .

Auden: "The arts are a chief means of communication with the dead. Without communication with the dead a fully human life is not possible."

Jim discussing the importance of Gertrude Stein, how when he feels overwhelmed by words, he goes back to her, to the individual word, to clear the ground.

But in my case I don't feel that words clutter me, on the contrary, I feel that I have to recreate them with difficulty out of thin air so to speak, their nature always too self-contained, too well defined, as if stone presences that constantly demand their singular places, demand that one should acknowledge their individual existence in relation to a meaning. I would feel that this repetitive, mechanical use means that I am letting them down, emptying them of their meaning.

AUGUST

At the opening, we arrived late, the gallery dense with people. For the first time in that sombre place a feeling of warmth. She as usual looking polite, warm and detached at the same time, in black, with that astonishing coloring of her skin, as if gold-dusted, and her red golden hair, dyed, the color somehow totally suited to the overall effect.

But he looked devastated, his curly hair shooting in all directions, as if Medusa's hair. His eyes very black with a desperation that he was trying to keep in check, his glass in hand, running after the waiter to fill it again. He was rushing to escape all these fires that were coming at him from all sides, laughing in a forced yet careless way.

The paintings large and sombre, an inner calligraphy that had acquired substance, black-blues, browns.

We waited for the dance to start, looking at the marvelous paintings. Seemingly simple, yet the details baroque, juxtaposing themselves in colors that miraculously dissolved into abstractions full of lightness.

It was raining heavily outside, visitors were coming and going, the women strong-bodied with large breasts, simple effective designs on them, moved slowly in the beat. A camera permanently recording them. Documentation has become the purpose of any event now. Before people talked about it, transformed it over the years into a story, a myth, but now the cold comfort of a camera only.

The young women with dark, beautiful skins, delicate heads and ascetic-looking hands.

The artifacts were exhibited in another room, a young boy began to play with one of the women's digging sticks, an elder came immediately to take it away from him, he put it back, was telling the boy in signs, of the potency of the stick, pointing to his head, as if some madness that would take over, throw him upward in some explosion. The magic potency of the women's tools.

Dream. Nighttime, the streets empty and very cold. Walking toward the back gate, suddenly in front of the wall—Mother was standing, small and dressed in brown. I was stunned, pleased, moved quickly toward her, stretched out my hand to touch her. As my hand went out she transformed into a transparent form that was immediately absorbed by the wall, a cinematic fade-out.

I stood there before the empty brick wall.

SEPTEMBER

Looking out of the terrace over the city, the warm haze, the orange tree full of buds, flowers, a strong scent in the air. He was asking me what I was working on, making jokes about titles, when I said—"Intimacy"—his eyelashes fluttered, as if the impact of the word was breathtaking in its immediacy and implications.

We came out through a narrow passage between the flats, a plane was coming into Mascot, riding just above our heads, in the dark gray sky, with a tremendous roar. This giant bridal bird, silver white, with a solid body illuminated from inside. The red and blue lights flashing in all directions, like some fantastic dream apparition, so close, so monumental, to disappear in a deafening sound.

Behind the gray veil the face of the moon was moving, the light yellow-gray, steamy.

OCTOBER

Dream—I was at a table with a group of people and there was the Devil. I had never dreamt of the Devil before. A short, thin man with cropped whitish silver hair and a vinegary, tight, constipated smile. Above his rather large ears, two horns, also whitish, as in the Romanian stories, but these were more visible, protruding just above each ear, from the skull. His voice, sounds of an indescribable quality that somehow underlined his nature, thin, sharp, with a sulfurous center. A sinister white light was falling on him and his skull seemed cut out of glossy silver paper.

When I woke up I realized it was one of the speakers on the panel in the TV show.

Very hot suddenly, the wind as if midsummer, a dove advancing on the garden path, swaying from side to side, going toward the water dish. The tree at the gate heavy with white flowers.

Sitting at the desk and looking at the garden, past the gate the grandmother pushing the pram, a large bird landing in the tree, opening its wings, splashing the air with a black sound.

Talking to Chitra last night, the illness, the treatments—fear traveling on the spring wind with the scent of the flowers.

They had left this trial packet of laundry powder in the letterbox. They described it in powerful terms—oxygen bleach, stains removed, dazzling whites . . .

They are still at their fifties best, selling us this elusive quality of "whiteness" that they still think women, "housewives," are constantly dreaming of. So behind the times. They don't realize that none of us gives a fig about whiteness—whiter than white—this metaphysical position, accessible, one imagines, to God only.

NOVEMBER

The bats eating the apricots at night, flying away, their wings like heavy cloth beating against the air.

One felt very sad after watching him on TV. A change of sex, a fixation with bodies, breasts, buttocks, and women's clothing. A fifties image of high heels, flared pink skirts, large rouged lips and so on . . . a tinselled sort of womanhood that he was trying to achieve. All these clichés created by Hollywood sentimentality which have come back to haunt him, to imprison him.

Reading the interviews with the French intellectuals—the photo of the structuralists—grim-looking and anorexic, probably they are flat-footed too, as Jimmy Durante would say.

We came home for coffee and talked about the literary scene in the fifties, when they had arrived here. How stratified it was, with certain names absolutely at the top of the ladder. Slessor for instance, the tones of awe in which everyone talked of him. But now another matter, J. felt, the whole scene had disintegrated in such small groups that no one could convincingly claim to be on top of the ladder.

J. thought that if there were such scales any longer, the ledges must be so narrow that one would have to have pigeons' feet to be able to hold on.

We all laughed.

Y. was getting very sleepy . . . she thought that some writers had very small feet.

DECEMBER

Eduardo Galeano was being interviewed about his trilogy—The History of the Americas. In the course of his research he came across a book written by a priest at the end of the nineteenth century. The priest was working with an Indian tribe. They asked him about the paper used for the holy book. What was paper? He was trying to explain to them, its purpose, you can use it, he said, to send messages to the people you love. The Indians went away, discussed how to name this new material in their language, finally came back. They had called it "the skin of God." Galeano was saying that he feels this summarizes the implications of the craft of a writer, his responsibilities—using the skin of God.

We went for a walk by the sea. Manly very beautiful at night. The sea made of some magnificent dark velvet cloth. On the line of the horizon a static boat and the moon raining down silver, a crystal path on the blackness, far away . . .

JOURNAL II

JANUARY

A heatwave today. Driving into a sea of hot air and light, the horizon dusted with the smoke of fires burning far away in the mountains. Mirrors everywhere, reflecting from the tops of cars, windows, the air sparkling as if made of particles of ice.

We came home and closed all the windows, the doors, drew the curtains, barricaded ourselves against the heat, then watched from inside the spectacle—this white burning stillness falling on everything.

After the heatwave, a big storm last night, shredding the trees, the wind moving in whirlpools above the streetlights. Late at night the wind subsided, the sky suddenly clear and this brilliant, miraculous full moon above the city, slightly off the Bridge.

An article about a retrospective exhibition of Max Beckmann's works. Max Beckmann describing colors as: "The strange and magnificent expression of the inscrutable spectrum of Eternity."

Wieniawski's *The Legend* over the radio, as of old. Father playing. This intimate, mysterious music traveling across time. The documentary on European musicians reminded me of him, all these short, compact men, with small energetic hands.

At Kate's for dinner. On the terrace, the sun was setting, the sea very still, a lake full of golden brown reflections. From the other side the sound of a motor.

Discussions about the new theories, the new discoveries, magnetic zones, a new phenomenon that could not be measured before, the instruments not fine enough.

At every age, the universe lends itself to us, graciously.

FEBRUARY

Touching the flowers of the bottlebrush, soft as the fur of a cat.

Hot and humid, storms during the night, the rain pelting down, the lightning, a spectral white-blue opalescence, flashing silently in the room. The thunder would come from far away, bursting on top of the house. Then the lightning again, sinister, flicked in and out by an unseen hand. I woke up afraid.

Reading Stendhal's autobiography *The Life of Henry Brulard*, he talks of writing: "We are all writing as if the world is attacking us, we are writing from a center that we try to make into a retreat from which we are going out to repulse the advancing armies of the enemies . . ." And later: "In the presence of people I loved, I totally lost myself, my personality."

At the pictures, sitting in the dark, couples, kids, elderly people, all of us watching this amazing intimacy shown on the screen. Before, this type of sexual intimacy would have been in books, a one-to-one involvement, but now a mass participation.

Albert Tucker in a documentary about his life, Joy Hester . . . "Women," he was saying, "have an insidious power to invade the male psyche, one has to be aware of it all the time." As if describing the enemy at the gate.

I was falling in and out of sleep, dreaming of Mother in the backyard putting clothes on the line, talking. I helping, making myself useful. The light on the clothes, brilliant white, peaceful, full of a live element, like the light for the last few days—luminous.

MARCH

Katherine Anne Porter: "Love is purely a creation of the human imagination. It is the most important example of how imagination continuously outruns the creature it inhabits."

A beautiful autumn day, the sky, a vast resonating chamber in which the planes are entering. Driving to our Sunday lunch, everyone in a good mood. We stopped on the way at an Italian delicatessen full of smells of goat cheese, dry figs, exotic Easter cakes in baroque-looking boxes, tins and tins of olive oils, pastas. We were all lost in these fields of possibilities—walnuts, coffee, mountains of bread.

Finally we made it to R.'s. The sea below dark blue, full of high waves and eerie-looking surfers in their black rubber suits, thin and tall, running, as if on hot coals, down the hill, with their surfboards.

After lunch we went down, the street very steep, the sea beating between two rock heads. Wild, dark, tall waves falling on the beach with a tremendous sound, turning into foam, a continuous activity, the sound so powerful we had to shout, and on the crest of the waves these black sea creatures.

When you look at Celan's anguish, yours becomes an affectation. But how can one live with such anguish? One has to read him at noon, with the sun out, friends in the house, to counteract this sort of desperation.

Bertolucci talking about films and filming. After all the preparations, when one is filming, it is a moment in the lives of the actors, the crew . . . when the scene is finished, the moment has passed forever.

He was quoting Cocteau: "The cinema is death at work."

Viv talking as always about Hindu metaphysics—stopping time, insinuating oneself in the momentary gap, tapping into the vitality of the universe, the potency of the cosmos. What an amazing notion. All this to be achieved through ritual.

APRIL

We left Canberra early in the morning, the mist was rising like steam from the ground. Around us the silence of the hills, the cows in the paddocks insubstantial shapes. Driving up the little bridge we took the wrong turn. The white gums tall and very beautiful, and suddenly in the middle of the bush this white clay mine. A mountain of clay of a startling old marble whiteness, above it the sky had become sharp blue.

We came out, walked around it, climbed it. The ground had been cut into a large opening with serrated walls, filled now with rainwater, a small lake that reflected the sky, transforming it into a giant boulder opal, turquoise blue.

We became very excited, took photos. The forest full of large gums, their bark marked by a cuneiform script. An ancient hand or some cardiac machine that had left its mark?

On the way back, we stopped in Goulburn, at the Paragon Café, for some tea.

When the ambulance went past, the dog next door started to howl, a human howl, as if it had released in him some deep anguish, a sound of mourning, of deep weeping, his head tilted upward, matching his voice to that of the ambulance.

Rereading Chamfort, his acid wit, his aphorisms, his despair at the terrible transformations of the French Revolution, his tragic end. His quotes: "Man comes to each age of his life a novice"; "It is only the uselessness of the first flood that keeps God from sending a second"; "In society you have three kinds of friends: your friends who are fond of you, your friends who don't care either way, and your friends who detest you."

MAY

A review of the latest book of the well-known writer, full of admiration, describing him as: ". . . a protean figure, the international literary superhero, Bard of the bush and champion of rural Australia, a polylingual translator, someone solemn, grand, eclectic . . ." and so on, then quoting a politician who referred to him as: "The Ayers Rock of Australian literature, central, vast, immovable, contentious and yet changing with the colors of the day . . ."

Admiration always sounds so absolute, so totalitarian. Afternoon visit to Mrs. Crawford. She was on the balcony with her straw hat, but complaining that she had lost again her front teeth. She was very pleased to see me. She kept looking at me with her still, aquamarine eyes.

From the balcony we watched the city and the new bridge. The milky light falling on the park, the garden next door, the lemon tree heaving under the weight of lemons.

I asked her if Linda Williams had come to see her. "Linda Williams," she said, the name was familiar, but she could not remember her. So many names that one had to place.

We seem to be slowly disconnecting from everything, things are receding further and further away, till we lose even the memory of something we can't place, the loss remembered vaguely at the beginning, later only a faint feeling about it, a light shadow absorbed by the everyday.

Discussions over the radio about Liszt and his career as a concert pianist. His impact on audiences was spectacular, on women, of course, but it was reported at the time, that after listening to him: "Even strong men became incoherent."

I rather liked that.

JUNE

Coming out of the Opera House, the city was rising lighted in the mist, weightless, the massive shapes of the buildings floating above the ground.

Discussing with I. the idea of size in literature. I felt that it has something to do with the physical space of the country, as in America too, people trying to cover it by inflating all things—oversized cars, buildings, novels, instead of concentrating them as in populated countries.

But the whole scene, it seems to me, quite impoverished, an age of salespeople, men and women, constantly tailoring their minds to one goal, how to sell and sell more, as if life, reality, growing up, dying, have anything to do with it.

These are forces outside the framework of these merchants, a melancholy kingdom totally sealed off and constantly giving itself prizes, more and more of them, in need of constant reassurance that they are the best, measure up against all the past masters, which they are simplifying for easy consumption, at any rate. Lists of past giants are constantly being prepared, for comparison.

Munch: "Like all nervous people I talk a lot. When I talk I confide in the person I am with and prevent them from attacking me. Some people use speech like gas to silence their victims and thwart their intentions, they use talk as a weapon for attack. I use it as a means of self-defense."

JULY

I had arrived too early. The new building a huge bunker, everything aluminum-colored, the walls, the furniture, people at the far end going up the escalator, puppets disappearing into the vast glass ceiling.

The convention hall was full of tables laid out with flowers and candles. In the semi-darkness an army of waiters in black with white gloves moved about.

They slowly began to arrive, the large black curtain wall parting as they came in. Then P. R. came to sit at the same table. He was astonished to see me there, looked at me as if an interloper in his familiar world. He proceeded to tell me of his involvement with the "ethnics," obviously the only topic of conversation with me. For the rest of the night he sat on the other side of the table, small and rather discolored, stunned in his own unease, smiling an embarrassed smile to the air, convinced that his success could not be that great if people like me were part of it.

Then the journalist approached, introduced himself, he seemed in a permanent hurry, a minor official at court, running with the excitement of some dreadful catastrophe befalling an important personage. He asked me in a breathless voice how was D.

As far as I knew he was overseas having a good time. "No, no," he said, he is back, had had a stroke and lost his eyesight. "Imagine," he said, "incapable of reading."

I was stunned, looked around to see if I could find him, black-clad figures were coming in, moving through the catacombian darkness, voices that were laughing, telling stories. Then the curtain parted and there was D. Tall, walking on the arm of his wife, holding himself erect with dignity. Later I went to say hello, he apologized for the dark glasses he was wearing, the lights bothered him.

We went on, seated now, to eat our entrées, objects with little taste, difficult to define their origins, and drink the next round of wine to the deafening sound of the slide presentation that had started.

When the second course arrived on the large white plates, a piece of chicken that had been forced into a perfect round form to appear as a rose in the middle of the potatoes, I asked my neighbor laughing: "Don't you think that we eat and drink too much for intellectuals?"

She cut me down immediately in a sharp voice: "This is a thirties idea."

Then the proceedings began, the Master of Ceremonies totally in control, but at ease. They all seemed very pleased with themselves, their products, their style, the sales, a mutual admiration society. The language was as if of beef exports, rising curves of sales, local and overseas markets, exhaustive thanks to the sponsors, anecdotes of meetings with the great, defined as sportsmen or politicians.

Patrick White would have been very displeased with us, he would have quoted again his Amazonian proverb: "Nothing is lacking, only what is missing."

The very large audience clapped enthusiastically from the darkness, as the heroes mounted the podium. Behind them on the giant screen, crudely colored books floated in a yellow-red liquid.

I was looking at D. tall and sombre with his silver hair, in the light of the candles, seemingly watching the scene behind his dark glasses.

Was he seeing anything?

At the cemetery, the sky empty, only a plane painted on the surface of the blue, suspended above the monuments on the hill. No one about but some Greeks. The same woman selling flowers in the shop, slightly older now.

AUGUST

In the Saturday papers discussion about the major publishing house up for sale, everyone lamenting its possible demise, the loss of major imprints etc. But the management described the sale in the new terminologies as: "STRATEGIC REFOCUSING."

Georgia O'Keeffe: "Where I was born and where and how I lived is unimportant. It is what I have done with where I have been that should be of interest."

Listening to the singer, I thought of that amazing sweetness that I discovered in Spain, an unimagined sweetness, that is yet not too much, the absolute, refined sweetness that still maintains a backbone, that travels from cakes, to oranges, to language, to the light and back again.

I went with Y. to the official opening. Inside the clean lines of the gallery, waiters in white gloves were serving champagne, holding the bottles at the right angle, like exotic fruit they were handling carefully, pouring out the nectar.

The place was full already, everyone in black, with de rigueur haircuts, in heavy black shoes, bending under the weight of aesthetic problems, but with a rather vacant look on their faces.

The officials, in dark, blue-gray suits, spoke of culture and excellence.

Only Richard Hall was getting slightly drunk, complaining mockingly about the changes in the gallery. Where was the magnificent *David and Bathsheba*? Or *The Charge of the Light Brigade*? Everything had been replaced by a bronze nude with breasts held up by tape to stand forward in such an unnatural manner.

When we left, he was sitting on the bench outside, in the misty yellow air, between the Greek columns, smoking. He opened a last eye on us, as we passed, mischievous and ironic.

SEPTEMBER

The Andrzej Wajda interview—Polish nationalism and symbols. Listening to him you were in Polishness, all the concerns, the approach, the silent irony, the burden of nationalism, Catholicism, all interrelated.

He was at home, at night, by the fire, with a cat hovering in the background, and around him one felt the darkness. A sad, somber face.

Defining his fundamental aim—trying to have an affinity with the reality around him and with tradition.

Very hot on the terrace, in the sun, as if summer, a haze over the city, everything blooming already, the orange tree heavy with blossoms and scent, and bees coming and going.

Stefan was coming down Martin Place, slightly thinner after his heart attack, paler. He was overwhelmed at seeing me, kissed my hands, kissed me on both cheeks, went into his usual little performance, how well I looked, "Unchanged, unchanged," he kept saying, "like the Acropolis." "I agree, I agree," I said laughing, "a ruin."

Here we were pretending as of old, he a debonair young man flirting with a beautiful woman, but he had to stop and draw breath often, as if a heart attack was imminent.

We talked of the old countries. The club empty now, he said, all his friends at Rookwood.

His eyes a faded brown, and his face longer and sadder under the elegant straw hat.

We went to see Patricia in a small role in the play, falling down effortlessly as Dame Maud, who had one glass too many between acts. She alone sustaining the essence of the play, amusing oddities of stage life, she seemed to have a past, quirky opinions which seemed related to experience, despite the rather superficial text.

And that amazing ability, that she had always had, to convince one that she is floating on stage.

OCTOBER

Raining and a slight wind, the trees moving as if shaking themselves under water.

Looking out of the window at the back lane, there was the small utility carrying away Mrs. Crawford's meagre furniture, the round table, the two cupboards, the small bedside table. It seemed such an impoverished ending, sad and vulnerable.

Three months and everything has gone, the house sold, and all these strangers moving in, with their furniture, their presence in her rooms, looking out of her windows, sitting on her balcony. One is stunned to see them there, taking over her property, her home, her place of refuge till the end.

Nothing remains, as we know intellectually, but to feel the process itself, when it happens, a terrible realisation.

The dinner in honour of the Australian journalist who lives in New York. A tall, glossy woman with red painted nails and a warm skin, eating well, in between running down the local scene. Sydney, boring galleries, little to see, in NY you can go and see a masterpiece any time you want.

Ah! I thought, these people who recognize masterpieces and are constantly looking at them.

She was full of an attacking energy, entertaining, constantly on the lookout for "politically correct victims," public money spent on useless projects, artists traveling to NY, an amplitude about her idea of money that she was bringing from NY, not realizing the paucity of the arts money here.

Then on to cooking . . . and how good Toklas and her cookbook were, but Gertrude, that heavy, stupid woman in the background . . .

I was listening to all this, could not find my way out of the maze of her perceptions.

NOVEMBER

The lady across the street is receiving visitors, an older woman holding a very small child. They are both bending over it, as if flowers in the wind. The child seems interested in the new surroundings, looking with curiosity at the garden, the street, the houses on the other side.

They both speak in babyish tones, one can almost hear them from the position of their bodies, their hands. They touch his fine hair, delicately.

In the film on Magritte, he was quoted as saying: "In my pictures, the spectator recognizes his isolation and listens to the silence of the world."

And later, commenting on his portrait with four hands: "The maniacs of movement and the maniacs of stillness will be equally disappointed."

Hot and humid this morning, last night a terrible electric storm. I waited for a long time for it to pass. The house hit constantly by blue, undulating lights, followed by a terrible cracking of the sky, as if the sky was made of heavy glass that was breaking on all fronts, on and on, the horizon lighting up with the flare of pale fires, ghostly fires.

Aboriginal storytelling, the landscape in the north populated with myths, the mountains, the rivers, the old woman saying:

> Through the singing we keep everything alive . . .
> Through the singing the spirits keep us alive . . .

Art too is constantly trying to sing the world alive.

Seferis writing to a friend: "The truth is one seeks not to get away from a place, not to travel, not to see again the people one loves, not even to create something. At bottom, one is seeking to get out of oneself, and perhaps the criterion of man's worth is the way he manages to get out of himself."

Elem Klimov's film—*Come and See*—on SBS. I was trying to escape it, who can face another film about the war and the Germans. But finally watched it. From the very first images he took you in, in the most subtle, unsuspecting manner, through the terrible events of the war. The film totally lacking in sentimentality, in brutalities, well centered. You were in it as if it were your own life unfolding in these fields scorched by the modern machinery of war. Friends you were talking to a moment earlier blown to shreds, the terrible signs of massacres everywhere, corpses, dead chickens piled up, flies, uncanny silences. The music score underlying all of this.

Everything achieved with enormous economy of means, the camera following people as if running with them, breathing with them. After the destruction of the camp in the forest, the stork walking with elegance, inquisitiveness and resignation somehow. The moon coming up, offering either danger or indifference.

Later I saw a documentary on Klimov, a human, lived face, his hands very expressive.

"What is man? The eternal question in art."

He lost his wife Larissa in a car accident, she was a film-maker too, she was returning with the crew after a shoot, when the accident occurred.

Photos of her, a beautiful, elegant woman. I had seen one of her films called *Ascent*, in black and white, also about the German occupation and death. The film as if a painting, the snow, small details that anchored it.

They were both filming from books. The film that he had to finish after her death was from a book by Valentin Rasputin. Klimov was saying how difficult it was to film it. Film, he said, is a brutal medium, how to match the poetry, the subtlety of the book, he made a gesture with his fingers as if trying to catch light through them.

DECEMBER

We walked down the empty, deserted streets, in the dusk, the cars passing down fast with a swishing sound. Most shops closed, only the delicatessen glowing in the night. We bought smoked herrings in Father's memory, remembered how he loved to prepare them, searing them on the flame, so that the skin became alive with a copper, golden glow.

In a review by Helen Vendler of Steven Axelrod's *Robert Lowell: Life and Art*: "There was a degree of controversy about the recent Mary Cassatt exhibition . . . the show juxtaposed domestic objects with paintings of the same objects—a tea set, a silver service . . . The good intentions of the exhibition, to bring art closer to biography and thereby closer to the viewer, begged, once again, the central question: What had the data become in the picture? Cézanne's bottles, cherub and skulls, stand untransfigured now in his studio, all light fled from them . . . Lowell's domestic and public data, his mother's Risorgimento coffin, etc., would not only not be art, they would also not be 'experience.' We cannot go behind art. The illusion that we can is of course art's most compelling hallucination."

Last night watching a TV performance of Handel's *Messiah* in Dublin. All these young women violinists in the orchestra, in their rich blue-green evening gowns, looking as if Mary's sisters. The same light brown hair, shoulders, but especially her elbows and hands. Rather naive, young and awkward elbows, diffident, but attacking Handel with vigor.

JOURNAL III

TRAVEL

In London at last. The journey a torture. Flying into this interminable day, this interminable night, with an army of people, all restless, trapped in our narrow allotted spaces, the children crying constantly, quarrelsome, desperate in the night.

Stopovers in dark cities, small people, guards, pop music over the loudspeakers, and the posters advertising American goods.

2 a.m. at Bahrain. Walking up and down the airport like lost souls. At one end, the heavy wooden doors of the mosque, and the city outside, just small lights in the distance.

In the corridors people asleep on benches, on the ground, children, women in colorful clothes, we smile at each other. Through the large glass windows, the carcasses of planes lying in the darkness, as if huge beasts, empty houses, the lights of the city flickering through their windows, mysteriously.

All modern airports now seem designed by the same architect using the same materials—steel, concrete, glass. Spaces that always look too impersonal and cold. Only this army of cleaners bringing a human element to them. One sees them everywhere, short women in overalls, moving with their mops and buckets. An international sisterhood, speaking to each other in foreign tongues, in the impersonal corridors, below the signs of forks, spoons . . . then disappearing silently absorbed by the distance.

LONDON

Walking through South Kensington, everything in pastel colors, the texture of the buildings, the streets spacious, yet a feeling of intimacy, all the trees full of delicate young leaves, leek green, very moving. The poetry of a great city, places humanized by living, by history.

The place full of tourists, other languages being spoken everywhere, a feeling of inclusiveness. Going out to buy the papers this morning, two well-dressed, short gentlemen stopped me to ask for directions.

I said that I was a visitor.

We all smiled good-naturedly at each other. One said in specific English—"I shall look for an Englishman."

It seemed a scarce commodity around here.

The hotel unchanged from the last time. The same windowless breakfast room with the very blonde girls behind the counter. Rather empty this morning, a few couples and women eating their toasts, and an African man with cropped black-bronze hair, a crumpled suit on and stooped shoulders. He ate with concentration, breaking the slices of bread in small pieces, then dipping them first into the butter, lying on the table in its foil, and then into the jam. He went on steadily, using his long, elegant fingers, not touching any cutlery. He had already gone through some four pieces of butter, but he asked for another one. The girls giggling behind the counter. Then he asked for a glass of water which he mixed with some milk, and he drank it.

One wondered what patterns he was repeating that we had not heard of, the whole room watching attentively, without showing it, in consternation, a tension about the room as if something was going to explode. How full of panic we are about everything. Uniformity the great stabilizer.

The Natural History Museum floodlit at night, pearl-blue gray behind the fine net of trees.

I am becoming attached to the building. Yesterday I went in again. A man with white hair, one stooped shoulder, walking as if on glass, went before me up the wide steps. One of those people with serious, absent-minded eyes, yet seeing you very well. One imagined a scientist in the fossils department. He climbed the steps with avidity and went in through a side door.

In the shop one can buy porcelain pandas, fossilized animals, books on zebras. When I came out long lines of school children were arriving, chirruping, with bright eyes, their drawing boards showing some prehistoric animal.

Outside the traffic was going past. In the distance the Victoria and Albert Museum encrusted with lime. Below the trees, a couple kissing, delicately. She one arm around his neck, an upturned nose, kissing his cheek, then his nose, an easy, familiar feeling.

This morning Alice and Peter came to give me a quick tour of the city. Regent's Park, Hyde Park, the Peking ducks with their marvelous deep apricot feathers, the imposing heads, then the pelicans.

At Buckingham Palace masses and masses of people taking photographs, trying to film the changing of the guards, these little men, they look infinitely more statuesque on television. They were playing little thin flutes and a drum equally tinny. But everywhere the spaciousness of the park, the gates, and the large statue of Queen Victoria, in her younger days, sitting well, with the winged goddess above, gilded, glowing in the full sunshine.

The trees in front of the Tate full of red cherry blossoms and inside, Cézanne's *The Gardener*, beautifully caught, the light through the leaves falling on him forever.

Back in London after the conference. I woke up at five o'clock, cool and cloudy. The birds in the empty vault of the sky exercising their vocal chords. The sound as of rubber gut strings. Large birds that came again and again to cry mournfully. An early lament over the city.

Very tired with so many people, faces, voices, papers. The closed nature of conferences, as of a club, a club of exchanged information, passing details, rough frameworks on which our lives could gain some order, make sense of an author, a book. A strange, killing exercise.

All this propaganda of books being published, geniuses at every corner, an inflated presentation that leaves one empty. Social realism everywhere and technical experimentation. English, infinitely seductive, and in spite of its lingua franca status, international inputs and so on, very closed in, not allowing for wider cultural truths. One realizes again how tight any cultural system is. One wonders what sort of conference it would have been in French, Italian, Japanese, Hindi.

The operative word is *postcolonial*, but it is the elite of the former empire, the most colonized of all that are struggling with it, using the language of the conqueror to do the analysis. Yet no one discussed language.

Trying to join a queue for lunch, uncertain where to go, the woman at the entrance of the cafeteria telling me in a loud voice: "Madam, this is a one-way system."

In the train, coming back, this friendly academic who had been to Australia, discussing Patrick White, while the train traveled on with its electric-blue covered seats and the dusty windows. The landscape outside, medieval England, small towns, cathedrals as in the old engravings, then industrial towns, followed by fields, waves and waves of them.

His voice low-key and careful, the place full of intellectuals speaking in reasonable voices, as if objectivity is in their blood. Their ultimate weapon.

VENICE

Suddenly we were in a water taxi, moving fast, water everywhere, the sun sparkling on it, gliding through a road marked by pillars bound together, dark figures embracing, consoling each other, planted in the sea.

Above us the buildings, cupolas in the strong light, figures flying in the air with their golden orbs, the bells ringing.

Walking to San Marco, the warm, lived nature of Italian cities, through narrow streets, as if fortified against the sea. The Piazza San Marco full of people and pigeons.

I went into the church, a dark, somber place, well spaced, the mosaics very beautiful, the marble walls as if made of moiré silk. In the treasury, Byzantine vases, glass, semiprecious stones, very delicate portraits painted on medallions of men looking like Nikos. Quirky Greek faces with the air of revolutionaries, but not as fierce as those of the Greek Independence War, more domesticated.

A scent of fried fish drifted through the Doge's Palace. Wide staircases, marble halls, ceilings decorated in fine sculpted wood covered in gold leaf. Political power everywhere and its exercise. The paintings full of men with heavy insignia of office, the women appearing mostly as allegorical figures.

Past the Hall of the Great Council, "the largest room in the world unsupported by pillars," the prison where Casanova stayed.

Tintoretto's "*Paradise*, the largest oil painting in the world." All this information from a guide taking a group of tourists around. A young man elegantly dressed, in white trousers and a green shirt, carrying *Time* magazine and an unlit cigarette in his hand.

Downstairs, an exhibition of pre-Columbian art.

Dark, high-ceiling rooms, powerful lights falling on the sculptures, mysterious figures, stocky and heavy, made of terracotta, smelling of blood sacrifices, impenetrable faces, their tongues out, physical deformations used to great effect, a raw energy working from inside them, some cosmic power, a silence in their faces, an indifference. The massive goddess with snakes around her waist, very alive, as if ready to talk.

The whole city a work of art, intimate, yet full of space and vistas. Having coffee in the Piazza San Marco with another hundred tourists, yet one does not notice it, nor is crushed by their presence.

All opera sets have come alive, one imagines conspirators coming out of dark side streets, preceded by a lean, silent cat.

I am staying at the pensione where Ruskin stayed. Venice grateful, a plaque to mark the building. Ruskin described as "Il sacerdote dell'arte."

An oppressively hot night. No air in the room. Late, American voices speaking loudly. The sounds amplified by the dry, wooden floors, reverberating as in a resonating chamber, as if in my room, in my head. Toward morning a smell of mud, sickly sweet, rising from the sea. Tired in the morning. Having breakfast downstairs I was watching through the window this immense cruiser gliding by, full of tourists, so huge by comparison with the buildings that it seemed to have grown in an Alice in Wonderland sea world, while we had remained small.

Then suddenly past the window, Paul was walking down the quay. I ran after him. What an amazing coincidence! Meeting in Venice! He was here for the Biennale. I very enthusiastic about Venice. Yes, yes, but terrible in winter, and the Venetians not very well organized . . . I laughed. They must have their own way of organizing.

In the evening we have dinner in a garden restaurant. He picks up immediately our old discussion in Sydney about Alan's suicide. How could it have happened? How come no one noticed? True, he was much thinner toward the end, but somehow he seemed to be his old self, joking, full of cutting ironies, in that supercilious tone, like a precocious child trying to annoy the grown-ups.

But I remembered well the last time I had seen him. I was in the bus in North Sydney. We had stopped at the lights. Late afternoon, the post office at the corner glowing with lights. As I looked down at the intersection, waiting to cross the street, this thin man with a moustache, familiar somehow, watching the street preoccupied, his limbs thin and slightly broken, yet putting on a sociable face, at the lights, the performance of a person ready to cross. He looked vaguely like Alan, yet altered, as if his essential nature had changed. The moustache a new addition to his appearance. I could only see his profile from the bus, I kept watching him. But as the bus started to move, he turned his head, it was Alan, yet a terrible alteration . . .

We walked back through dark, silent, narrow lanes, our elongated shadows traveling before us, few lights, no sounds from inside the houses.

The Venetians a most discreet people.

This morning I walked to the Biennale, pleased again with the easy elegance of the houses, the intimate squares, the tomato paste façades. The quay full of tourists and children crying. Yet what is noticeable is the absence of loud music, transistors, except when foreign kids let them loose in narrow streets and the locals look displeased at this display.

Past eleven, the light already falling powdered over the monuments, the vendors selling beads, marvelous glass beads, mother-of-pearl, amber, Egyptian blues . . .

The Biennale in the Giardini del Castelo. The place full of pavilions and demagogic architecture. The set for a Lina Wertmüller film, but here no irony. The German pavilion called "Germania—The House of No Weapons." Third Reich lines, heavy columns with a statue of Germania on top. The Italian pavilion as if designed by Mussolini. Inside, brutal spaces in which the works did not feel at ease. The most interesting, the Japanese Pavilion, showing Toya Shigeo, a forest of wooden columns, trees, semi-abstract, well-sustained pieces, restrained and powerful. Ochre-brown, as if after an atomic devastation, winter maybe, yet bearing up to all this, sad and dignified.

The Czechs interesting too. Modern installations, terrible disasters, things eaten away by torture machines, disintegration.

After a while I became tired. Left. Walked back to the Arsenale, where the Biennale of the Young was showing. In this huge, impressive building with round columns, high ceiling, whitewashed walls, the young of all countries proved what a terrible thing an international style can be. Somehow the same mean, hard, technical language. A terrible emptiness took hold of me as I watched these three tripods on which rested three white boxes oozing out a faint smoke and a woman's voice reading a dictionary: "Bruxelle, barbue, belgique, borace . . ."

I came out. Waited for the vaporetto. On the steps of a closed church a young man was sitting, smoking, preoccupied with some inner problem, floating. A beautiful young head. Later I saw him walk past the Arsenale, his limbs as if broken.

I had my photo taken in front of San Marco. Waiting for the photographs to be developed, the back streets full of buildings in ruin, stale water, pigeon droppings, a decrepitude looked on with resignation. Even the lion representing Venice, as if a middle-aged person.

In the church of San Moise this morning, a woman was saying her prayers. I lit a candle for our dead, sat down to rest.

A man of excessive religiosity came in, nervously crossing himself in front of the idols, doing obeisance, holding on to a beret, adjusting his bag over his shoulder. He advanced with trepidation toward the open door next to the altar where the chief was talking to some important personage, he put out his hand humbly and at his constant disposal. He was told to wait. He put his beret and his papers in front of an idol. Was that proper? He genuflected in front of it, crossed himself, wiped his forehead, waited nervously. He approached the altar, did his obeisance there as well.

The tall man in civilian clothes guarding the church, clearing the burnt candles, moved about, as interested in the performance as myself.

Finally he was called in. Do they know each other, the Venetians, or is there some room for discoveries, unknowns?

In the mornings on the Zattere the men and the boats are at work. And on the steps of bridges everything is being carted with great effort—furniture, food, rubbish, this is what keeps them thin, their tempo is also at ease, yet rapid.

Coming out of the museum I had lost my way. I asked a young woman passing by how to get to San Marco. She was all in black. An unforced elegance, black shoes, and dress, and a white belt. We walked briskly through the narrow lanes, turned corners, yet again in passages that would be dark at night, past bridges, a man smoking, leaning out of a top window, bored, sad. A small piazza with people, tourists, vegetable stalls. She walking with ease but quite fast and I almost running to keep up with her, and then miraculously she pointed to an opening and I was on the quay near San Marco.

Anthropomorphic forms everywhere, on the buildings. Gondolas lying, moving in green glistening backwaters, between buildings, like giant, brilliant black beetles.

Sunday. At San Marco this morning. The church full, the service, the sermon through microphones. Rhetorical voices talking of sacrifice, the divine, eternal life. When the mystery of the transubstantiation came, his voice whispered through the microphone while the worshippers knelt in silence. Then the triumphant raising of the wafer: "Il mio corpo . . . Il mio sangue . . ."

Then they all got up and drank it, ate it, came back on tiptoe, sat down, concentrating on this eating which they hoped would transform into good stuff. Abstracted cannibalism, a progression, one assumes, from earlier religious sacrifices and more ancient eating habits.

The outside walls of the cathedral full of magnificent mosaics, simple, immediate, well resolved, full of amazing visual angles, like beautiful naive paintings. The animals, small hills topped by trees, exotic trees on fire. The enthroned Mother of God looking preoccupied and stern, the child uncertain, as if focusing on something it was trying to decipher. Byzantine mosaics. The Mother and Child interesting, not pretty, static, as with the later Renaissance ones. The Mother of God had the Greek writing—Mitera Theou.

The light in Venice filtered through a gauze, falling on us, turning everything dark golden. In the silence of the afternoons the sound of water splashing, boats, and these guttural, rocky Venetian voices, resonating inside caves, hidden chambers. The clocks chiming.

I have become very fond of the city. Going out in the coolness of the morning, the sea, the wooden poles in the water, three every time, embracing each other, the intimate squares, the few trees, the delicate pink glass street lamps.

Past the cemetery yesterday where Stravinsky and Diaghilev are buried. A grave in the middle of the sea, permanently listening to the rhythm, the sound of water.

ATHENS

Coming down into Athens, the airport small, modest, the sea a sheet of silver metal. Platinum light. On the other side the massive hills, friendly presences in lavender gray.

The same white houses, dusty streets, the low pines, and the olive trees shimmering velvet green.

Hot in Constitution Square. The guards at the Unknown Soldier changing, these tall, handsome young men in foustanelas. Crowds looking on, pigeons everywhere and tourists taking photographs. In the middle of the crowd, against the white stone wall, a priest in his black, flowing cassock, holding a pigeon for a little child, while the mother took photographs. It is as if the National Tourist Bureau is placing the right picture, in the right spot, for maximum effect.

Yesterday we went with Eleni to hear a Finnish soprano in the Cycladic Museum. A very elegant, cool place. White polished marble everywhere enhancing the transparency of the exhibit cases.

The recital in a small garden at the back, between apartment blocks, trellises, greenery. The acoustics not that good, but the soprano young and with a good voice. The music more immediate and moving heard in such an enclosed, intimate space. As if we were part of the physical effort to produce the sound, fighting with the singer over that marvelous aria from the Force of Destiny . . . Pace . . . Pace . . . It was late afternoon and above the garden the sky was changing colors, the lights going on in the apartments above us.

Before we left we went again around the museum. In the semi-darkness the goddesses were waiting in their lighted cages, their arms folded, hugging their bodies, a desperation they were trying to contain, their shoulders falling in a gesture of resignation.

Who were they?

Maybe women waiting on seashores for the return of men out at sea, in these dangerous waters, constantly sang in the old ballads:

Oh Sea
your hunger
has not abated yet . . .

Coming back in the bus in the middle of the heat, the trees as in the Byzantine frescoes in San Marco, small, awkward, on fire.

The bus full of people, unshaven, tortured by life, hanging from the straps. A strong country. Difficult. One can see it in their faces, as if they have carried stones, marble up the unending hills, not only with their hands, their bodies, a carrying that has marked their heads, their faces, deep furrowed, their eyes faded by the strong sun, the white dust.

We went to see Nikos this afternoon. The street, his house as if coming out of the paintings he was doing in Melbourne, at Abbotsford.

We looked at the new work coming to Australia for his next exhibition. Landscapes mostly, more abstract, subtle colors in yellows and golds, fields full of hazy summer light.

In his study, a few paintings of his earlier series. His fruit. I remembered well watching them in the silence of the gallery in Sydney, these marvelous, giant, metaphysical fruit, floating on apocalyptic backgrounds. Cherries, quinces, pears, plums made of volumes of color, substantial yet full of lightness. Rich reds, blues, dark grays, purples, colors of the imagination.

Nikos was telling us stories about Mt. Athos. Walking to Agia Lavra with two friends, one late afternoon, their heads traveling above the clouds as they climbed . . .

But suddenly from the street outside, the sound of flutes, drums. We all came out. A wedding party was going down the street, music, dancing, clapping of hands. The bride in a full-length brilliant white satin dress and a satin hat, beautiful dark eyes and skin, the groom in white too, with a round hat on which paper money had been stuck.

In a magazine, an article about the "Miracle Maker of Patission."

A young man, his portrait on the wall, painted in folk colors with a halo. Around him, in the small room, they were waiting to hear about the miracle, that was coming . . . that should come . . .

At the Archaeological Museum again to look at the superb statue of Poseidon. He was waiting for us, floating on air with outstretched arms. If you look at his face a slight smile on his lips, but in profile, totally serious, looking infinitely younger.

Reading the papers, discoveries of more antiquities while the underground is being built. One large statue that has just been put together. We are told that the statue was burnt at the front from the fires of the Persian Wars. The ultimate in terms of everyday reference.

Religion here more in evidence. A constant struggle to counteract unseen, fatal circumstances that the old gods, the current gods might bring about. Rituals now transferred to television.

At Zonars for my usual coffee. Faces à la Cavafy, smoking, drinking, reading the papers. Elderly gentlemen like

Father, with their hats on. Women in hats too. Discreet discussions about weddings.

A feeling of old-fashioned ease, polished furniture, through the glass windows people walking down Panepistimiou. Seferis was waiting here for his wife Maro who had gone to deliver his famous letter against the Dictatorship in 1968.

At Hydra for the day. I always think of the island in terms of the Australian group—the Johnstons, the Nolans.

A beautiful place. One forgets the long and continuous history of these places, the landscape still at ease with its past, carrying it lightly.

The same silver light everywhere, the deep blue of the painted doors, the windows, the seeming smallness, intimacy of the place, yet the harbour full of boats, small, large, very large with hundreds of tourists, and earlier warships.

In the newly opened Maritime Museum, the battle for the 1820 Revolution started here. On the wide staircase the portraits of the so-called "fire throwers," because they used old boats, filled them with gunpowder, set them on fire and sent them toward the Turkish fleet where they exploded.

All handsome, hard men with moustaches, the portraits on ceramics, some of them by Tsarouhis, the well-known painter. Their names . . . Miaoulis, Koundouriotis . . .

Hydra, so much history, as if a paring down of the landscape, stones mostly. History, history everywhere, ancient times, Byzantine times, Turkish occupation, the Revolution and so on. What moved me also were the proclamations at the time, the language full of the echoes of the French Revolution.

Lunch—peasant salad, octopus, calamari, bread and a lovely rosé wine. The houses on the hill looking as in Tuscany, a light gray, lavender color.

The nets along the quay a magnificent golden brown. On the radio, a woman's voice responding to an interviewer: "And who will defend the people from the burning breath of current events?" I rather liked it.

And later a man discussing the recent loss of a soccer match: "The loss last week, still an open wound."

The taxi driver, as we came home, a middle-aged man with long white hair, energetic, with a loud voice. He was plunging the old battered car down the narrow streets full of parked cars, out into the main road, talking of recent blackouts, high winds, trees uprooted, their heavy roots still by the roadside.

Something wild in the Greeks, one forgets it.

Over dinner, discussions about inner developments, religion. However, this idea of purity, in itself not only a difficult concept, but to a certain extent creating an entire field of impurity around itself, as a sustaining element.

This quest for purity, religious ecstasy, the emptying of Zen, something that I was never convinced of. States that can be attained briefly, but should one work so hard to reach them? Another type of pleasure maybe?
Eurydice took me to the Historical Museum in the Old Parliament House. An elegant, somber building that housed the first Parliament after the Revolution.

The place full of marvelous things, paintings, watercolors, portraits of all the heroes of the Revolution, Makriyannis looking splendid in his rich clothes, beautiful weapons. Swords, silver pistols, jewelry, miniature size New Testaments, with filigree covers, two centimetres in size, which the fighters carried with them. Hand-sewn flags of battles. One came out full of revolutionary fervor and feeling very patriotic.

But what this accumulation underlines constantly, is the amazing amount of energy, persistence, sacrifice, in the final analysis, so many deaths, for any occupation or oppressive political regime to be defeated. And how destructive these regimes are intrinsically, not allowing for an inner development of the place and its people, pressing them into an artificial obedience, direction, so that even after the liberation, so much energy has to be spent in recovering one's balance, retracing one's own line of development.

Looking at the intimate streets, the low pines, these black figures appearing and disappearing in the distance, it is the women that wear black constantly, as if they are the conscience of the place, the living memory of the dead. Men seem to be excluded from the duty.

In the plane. Suddenly in a sea of English, pouring out of the intercom, the TV, the flight attendants.

The long haul. We are already somewhere near Tashkent, where Akhmatova and Nadezhda Mandelstam lived during the war.

Food is being served. Across the aisle we smile at each other. "Are you holidaying in Sydney?" she asks.

"No, I am going home." A slight surprise in her face. "Home to Sydney."

When we finally arrive, we fly over the Opera House, the Bridge. I am very pleased. I am pleased with the blueness of the sky. I am pleased as if I had a hand in making the place.

JOURNAL IV

JANUARY

The full moon for the last few days, traveling through the night in all her splendor, veils of cool glass chips, and the city lying low, very low, the space suddenly grown higher, the perspective of a cathedral.

Writing—constantly trying to recapture the living element at the beginning of the experience, an elusive element that has to be recreated constantly by discovered means that will bring it out. A process which seems far removed from the experience itself, grounded in the medium.

Looking at his letter, nothing in common with him any longer, nothing, as I knew from the beginning, was afraid of. Why did I not stop then?

Always the grip factual events have on me, in some immediate way, as if grasping them to convince myself of their reality.

The party in James's garden. The sea at night, with the small bridge lighted sombrely, the shore on the other side, faint lights. We were eating in silence seated at the tables under the lantern lights.

Very late the painter arrived with a large group. He looked like a small monkey with large blue eyes and white hair. They were all very drunk, with perspiring faces, and the drink spoke through them in exactly the same way. They seemed to have lost their personalities, their gestures heavier, their eyes moving slowly in their heads as if made of water, their tongues struggling over large waves, unable to get over them, their voices loud and aggressively mean in the mysteriousness of the garden.

It was as if Circe had touched them with her stick and they had all become what they were in their innermost being.

FEBRUARY

The same people bending over the tables in the Library. The stained-glass windows in their usual places and the Greek inscription on the back wall.

When I came out it was evening, the sky still blue and very transparent. In front of the steps, the lights were burning on the black stems of their columns. The fountain on the other side cooling the air, the palm trees, their long feathered leaves, in the distance above the Bridge.

The magic of the city in summer, at dusk, holding your breath. The smell of the empty streets, the post office clock glowing in the night . . .

My type of country.

Rilke: "Works of art are of an infinite solitude, and nothing is less capable of reaching them than is criticism."

"Physical desire," she said, "is like yawning, so to speak. The more people you see yawning, the more you yawn yourself. It transmits to you, enlarges, remains in you, in your eyes, in your breath, in your imagination, more potent than the actuality."

One can hear the tick-tock of the clocks in the city, so stunned the silence. Nothing moves. The light falls as if refracted on dull metal that absorbs its sheen, then sifts over the city.

Rain has been predicted.

MARCH

Louis Armstrong on race relations: "A note is a note anywhere, a note has no color."

Pouring since yesterday, the tail end of a cyclone. Enormous amounts of water coming down steadily, as if it would never end. The lines of the city have disappeared and the landscape looks cozy, one street with houses swimming in the water, together with the trees, up to their knees deep.

They came late on Sunday night. He seemed thinner, his eyes very dark. A dark, warm presence. She, a clean look, articulate, but her hands, her hands bothered me. Hands capable within limits, but tending to some fixed intellectual or moral ideas. Afraid, but not recognizing the fear there.

He seemed rather detached from her, although they seemed to be sharing a lot of things, going together to yoga, readings, walking, apart from sharing a bed. He described her as "the girl I am living with at the moment." Before, he was saying that the "heat" in him is not matched by the women he meets. No one can find the same temperature anywhere.

At last the rain has stopped, for the moment at least, the sun has come out. The terrace boils, steam rises steadily in the distance over the city and the trees have filled with birds. They jump from branch to branch, hang on, move in a shower of drops.

Everything is slowly drying out, the grass, the sky, the trees, the people. Things hanging on the line, wet rugs, curtains, people sweeping in their doorways, the pavements. A little wind blowing.

A quote by Ionesco arrived with her letter: "If one does not understand the usefulness of the useless and the uselessness of the useful, one can not understand art. And a country where art is not understood is a country of slaves and robots . . ."

Ola speaking about her aunt, the anniversary of her death. Everything had been trimmed away when I saw her, ten years ago. An unsentimental attitude to life, like a straight, hard flame burning. Very well mannered, she drove me home, spoke of the man who taught her to drive in Poland, before the war.

The writer rang the other night. Discussions. He was sure that he will be recognized in time.

"When one is convinced of what one is doing," he said, "recognition must follow."

I was listening to all this. Yet time may have other ideas, different from ours.

APRIL

We went to spend a weekend at her house. A spacious, well-appointed place, slightly showy. A glossiness that had to be maintained. An illusion of grand living. But restful and full of warm colors.

They were both tense, pretending to be at ease. Only the boy moved between them, a thin boy with very blue eyes. He circled around us full of the boredom of childhood, moving from spot to spot, trying to engage us. But the grown-ups absorbed in themselves.

Outside the house, the tall, ash-blond gums whispered continuously in the wind. The cockatoos flew like arrows at level with your eyes, shrieking. Everywhere birds talking and insects, the sea shimmered in the distance, and the moored yachts moved as if toys.

The surface of the pool was very blue, in the strong light a stark mirror. And the little boy kept collecting worms from the bottom of the pool with a net, bringing them laboriously to the surface and then testing their bodies with his finger, if too soft, they would not revive, but if firm, placing them on the space between the tiles, maybe the sun will bring them to life.

I was reading an article by Gore Vidal on Tennessee Williams. Very cool, self-possessed, witty with an edge of sarcasm, preoccupied with small matters, but pretending that he was concerned with important things. And on the other side Tennessee Williams, short, flabby, with a moustache, obsessed with the gentility of his mother, one imagined that he had decaying teeth, the profile of a queen, and a smell of decadence about him that he tried to hide with cologne. But even from the article, Tennessee was preferable to Gore, he seemed more human, vulnerable like all of us. Gore's prose a refined journalism, hitting the truth now and again, nice to watch once, as in the TV interview, a performance with superb aplomb, but rather hollow.

Patricia in town, she came for lunch, warm, with that expressive mobile face, the large generous mouth and the blue eyes. The blue of Greek ceramics.

Describing a performance: "The role sat well on her." Actors: "an instrument that shapes every role, you are the instrument after all."

She kept talking about "pauses," how they are never given their importance, everyone destroys their effect by movement, instead of allowing them to make their impact in silence.

Wynton Marsalis talking about the blues: "Something to get you through the day, the night, with some style."

And: "Living in New Orleans gives you a sense of the fantastic."

MAY

Nadezhda Mandelstam in *Hope Against Hope*: "One imagines that for a poet auditory hallucinations are something in the nature of an occupational disease."

At the airport. U. going away. A woman from the Tourist Bureau approaches with a questionnaire, asks U. if he is a tourist, and he: "We are Australians, don't you recognize us?"

We should all paraphrase Satie: "Of course I am an Australian. At my age what do you expect me to be?"

Picasso's prints at the Art Gallery. Strong lines, his animals simple, solid, vivid, the bull's head, the owls, the frogs as if made of green spangles, breathing in a heavy earthiness.

Yet a sentimental approach when expressing relationships, the same heavy minotaurs greedily watching the same young, sleeping nudes. Static obsessions.

We drove out to visit Annette. The day very beautiful, crisp and sunny. Between the blond ochre color of the empty paddocks, a lonely horseman appearing suddenly, stopping, as if coming from some mysterious destination.

At Annette's the intimate old house, surrounded by ancient trees, gardens. Annette vulnerable-looking, not saying much, pleased to see us, setting the table, bringing things to eat. Friendly discussions in the dining room with the round table and ancestral portraits on the walls.

In the afternoon we went to feed carrots to the donkeys, the dogs running in front of us, excited.

And then behind the donkeys, in their gray-brown velvet coats, this black bull appeared. Massive-looking, with jet black eyes, looking at us from inside full of curiosity, friendliness, young, Annette said, in spite of its size.

He seemed like a flamenco dancer, a rock singer, some dark flamboyance in his presence, while the sun was setting over the open horizon and ibises were flying up from the lake.

JUNE

In the documentary Bergman was discussing his approach to filming. There is one right way in which a scene must be shot and one must try and find the shot. I remembered Fellini who said that the position of the camera is a moral angle. At the office going up and down in the lifts, meeting the same people, lost souls in a metallic pit, electronically operated and alive with muzak.

In the afternoon we saw Jean's slides from her visit to China. The archeological exhibition, the Winter Palace, the Temple of Heaven. A meticulous type of excellence, no nails in the building, thirty thousand joints, or some such thing. Then the first of May celebrations. The spring too cold, no flowers on the trees, so they closed all the parks and put artificial blossoms on the trees. The Ministry of Culture is also the Ministry of Propaganda.

At long polished tables, under elegant chandeliers, on platforms, in front of crowds, looking into cameras, speaking into microphones, the rulers of the world, these middle-aged men, in well-cut suits, ties, with drained faces . . .

The colors at night are magnificent. It grows dark very early, the sky full of vibrant reds, and then blues, dark, midnight blues that come over the city and on the Bridge, from the bus, one notices the weather vanes. I am very fond of weather vanes, delicate, iron arabesques, traveling light, but some resilience about them.

Rain at Newport. In the car waiting, looking at the streets. An elderly man like Father, going home with the shopping. The pine trees in the distance and the cars rushing. Opposite a real estate agent. Why real? To distinguish it from the imaginary, one assumes. Philosophical nuances.

JULY

Last night we watched a documentary about migrants going to the USA last century. They looked just like us, the smell of people that are thrown together and lose their individuality but are seen by others and finally by themselves as a mob.

They begin to have the same look, dishevelled, desperate, indifferent, move listlessly, with identical gestures, and have out of the same inner states the same reactions. I was seeing us in the fifties, on all these faces looking out of all those ships going to America.

I went to see Sarah at the workshop. She was working on a lithograph. The atmosphere very friendly. We had afternoon tea with hot raisin toast. They were turning the handles of the printing press, like spikes, and their gestures, as they turned them one by one, ancient gestures of women spinning, men turning wheels.

How ancient our gestures are, one sees them inscribed on marble or stone century after century.

At the Arts Centre for lunch. All the officials were there. The well-known journalist sat opposite me. Tall with reddish hair, a head carved by Mexican Indians, strong jaws, small eyes, ironic tone, sharp and cruel. A smile that shaped only his mouth, his eyes and face remained untouched. Each name I put forward, he immediately shot it down with some irony.

The air around his conversation sterilized and he picking up the corners with forceps, eyeing them carefully, having sprayed them with some chloroform, matter that kills the nerve.

When we left, he was walking down the street, his long wooden legs unbending from the waist, his rock-made head advancing with ease.

George Dennison in an article on "The Moral Effect of the Legend of Genet": "Nothing in these books is more moving than the confrontation in which nothingness seems to be answered chiefly by the will toward beauty, and of course this is not 'outside the world,' but it is quintessentially human. Sartre misses precisely this meaning of the act of art, that is, the authenticity, to use his word, of the pursuit of form."

AUGUST

The moon rising over the bridge last night
perfectly round
perfectly still
perfectly white.

At the Opera House to hear *Lakmé* by Delibes. An effervescence of sound, water jets, the sun passing through them transforming them into birds of paradise tails, filigrees of enormous delicacy and transparence. Explosions of sound that seemed to be maintained by refined forces that constantly took you in.

Mamush in her last letter: "To be afraid that your next breath might be your last."

In the dream I had gone to visit Isak Dinesen . . . She took us through a room full of dust and broken objects, to an enclosed veranda. Through one side of the windows we were above the open sea, in a mid-afternoon light. And on the other a lake of black water in which people were swimming, in fact not swimming but floating, immobile, some of them face down, although no one seemed desperate, they were just lying there in waters that seemed as at the spa, at the Salt Lake, black mud with a shine to it, the surface misty somehow.

Then we walked along the length of the corridor and came into a room equally dusty, full of broken marble bodies, their limbs strewn everywhere.

Very cold, raining the whole week, thinking of death, Charlie Smith hit by a car at night, lying in the street till the morning, kept alive so that his mother can come and see him.

Tall, thin, with perfectly white hair, in his well looked-after clothes. Flamboyant sometimes, wearing a red carnation in the office. Blue eyes, a youngish elderly man.

• • •

"Waiting. Waiting," she said. "Waiting for some indescribable happiness to come. Some sign of warmth from someone. Oh God! Why don't you cure me of this waiting."

But as Nadezhda Mandelstam said: "Waiting is a sign of hope, which shows that you are functioning as a human being."

SEPTEMBER

The first day of spring. The bulbuls on the electricity wire, talking to each other in exciting voices, moving their orange tails with swift gestures, their plumed hats. The fig tree in the garden next door full of new leaves, slightly bent ears sticking out of the dry twigs, tender green.

The garden full of small leaves pushing each other in their hurry to come out, the roses, dark red wine leaves, the silver gum microscopic leaves of the most delicate violet and the apricot, a magnificent golden green, so youthful that it catches your breath every time the sun passes through it.

The bronze statue of Poseidon in the Archaeological Museum in Athens, photographed on the cover of the magazine. The man with outstretched arms, his body perfectly balanced at a point where the idea of weight becomes superfluous, flying becomes more appropriate, the lightest grace about him, yet full of strength, his presence arresting, creating in one a sense of beauty. What Brancusi has described as: "Le beau c'est l'équité absolue."

Xavier Herbert in a documentary on TV, very subdued, with young eyes, not the talkative, exuberant Herbert we all heard about. Preoccupied with the interviewer and the camera, maybe. He seemed very lonely. He said that if he cannot do anything positive from now on, he will probably send his shadow to the caves, like the Aborigines.

OCTOBER

The weatherboard classroom full of paintings, strange animals with red burning eyes in a forest of blossoming trees. Black cocks made of paper with thin bodies and ribbons for their head feathers and children everywhere waiting silently, a transparent, full-of-light world waiting.

Then the clown appeared. They liked him, watched how he made himself up, and then directed him, how to place a chair properly so as not to fall, how to sit, accepting the character implicitly, even though the transformation had taken place before their eyes.

In the motel, on the eighth floor, with a view of the park, the massive gates, the lamppost lights, bluish, lost among the trees. A peaceful view as if a European city. From the window the people looked small, waiting at the lights, passing cars, empty intersections.

Then a light rain started, falling unheard, the pavements black, full of liquid lights shimmering in patches. When night came, the place full of sirens, ambulances, police, fire engines rattling through the high buildings, screaming demented down the street like strange animals.

Inside, the plumbing sizzled, beat against the pipes and from upstairs the muffled steps of the giant moved nervously between the bed and the window, again and again, a restless soul pacing in the night.

I kept thinking of the poem by Palamas that Father had set to music, "The Haunted Palace":

and when night falls
a hoarse voice
comes as from a tomb . . .

Father coming off the plane on Monday, his trousers too long, his overcoat faded. More fragile than last time. Rather vague.

I went to visit John in his new place. A nice, warm, old house, with a terraced garden right down to the sea. The level of the water high, as at Heraclion, you felt like shooting your palm across it.

He was still full of his usual quirky ideas, his latest hypothesis about the genesis of the sexes, a fully worked theory using the Greeks as the basis. At the beginning there were only women and from them came men, why otherwise would men have breasts too?

He was expanding this entire theory to me while beating the cream, frying the fish, keeping an eye on the sorrel soup. Preoccupied, looking at you with his green melancholy eyes, responding only partially to your presence. Talking about his students. That beautiful young man he had fallen for. He wondered if he were still as beautiful.

Gray overcast sky through the bedroom window. A dove perched delicately on the electricity wire. The smell of roasted chicken from downstairs and the sound of the radio.

NOVEMBER

Raining and a slight wind. The trees moving as if shaking themselves under water.

Talking with Mother about growing old. These physical transformations that always astonished her, as if at each step another person unrelated to you is taking over, transforming constantly into this new being. The moment you become adjusted to it, it has already moved toward another transformation.

On TV a family of elephants walking leisurely in the dry, dusty bush. Then suddenly—the killers. The first one fell, the group rushed forward, unafraid, prodded him with their trunks, talked to him, raised their heads, their trunks, their ears in lamentation, let them fall on him, touched him with their trunks, moved like people in mourning, tearing their veils, falling on the dead.

She insisted that I must come to the party, in the new house she had just bought. It will be great fun, great fun. Saturday afternoon. I bought a flagon of white, took a taxi. The afternoon very hot and windy. The streets full of leaves, papers, rubbish everywhere. The houses in the street looked decrepit with children playing on dismembered couches lying on front verandas full of flaking paint. The tree in front of the doctor's house had been mutilated beyond recognition, short, thick arms, stubs against the bare façade of the house in the afternoon light.

The taxi driver was dark, with a moustache, he looked Greek, his hair was brilliantined, pasted down and swept in a roll that cut the back of his head in two.

We searched slowly for the address, in empty streets, at the back of factories, we went down narrow alleys facing railway yards, soot on everything and dust, houses with migrant women in open doorways, looking forlornly at the street, children playing under trucks.

Finally we found it at the corner, a tall, thin house with a shop front. The door was open and people were sitting on the floor. The place full of unknown faces as I went through the kitchen, the narrow yard, looking for P.

She was there with her hair dyed blonde and a transparent blouse on. But the small back garden smelt of some dark hole. The two walls were peeling and the fence was of corrugated iron. It was as if some dark soul was moldering away in the place. Everybody looked uncertain of their bearings, dressed in their de rigueur outfits, badges on their lapels, holding plastic plates on which the remains of some black beans were left.

We seemed to be in a burial ground in the middle of corrugated iron ruins, and all these lost souls, drinking out of plastic cups, the men with thin chins, fifties crew cuts and shirts with Hawaiian palms.

Biological time, biological rhythm. Everything moving at different time spans, from birth, to breathing, to lovemaking, to musical rhythms, to fever, to agony. The universe a giant musical machine, full of force and subtlety and we trying to catch the rhythms imperfectly.

DECEMBER

I left the office early. The city like a furnace, waves of hot wind rising and blowing over you, sweeping like surf. The pavements burning, the trees wasted in the heat, the surface of the sea fanned dark green by the winds. The bus full of wet faces. The cars coming from the angle of the street, undecided somehow, fighting the sheets of glass, as if topless cars, only the wheels and a ball of fire above them.

Martin Place was teeming with people, the trees full of glowing Christmas decorations, the benches full, the fountain, somber gray marble, the water coming down in a glass-like wall. In the small amphitheater the band was playing New Orleans jazz, soft melodies with a strong rhythm. The players in black trousers and white shirts. The sun pouring down on the concrete, the people, the thin trees, the faces of the musicians.

The new buildings full of that rough, mock elegance that we seem to give to most things. A gutsy vulgarity that imagines itself refined, sparkling in the hot sun in Glomesh splendor, tinseled windows, imitation ancient tiles . . .

But I felt quite optimistic, all this energy that fancied itself appeared somehow benevolent under the sun.

People were always afraid of this intensity in her, they did not feel at home in it. Something strange, that you could have a little of, at intervals, when you felt like some excitement, but not all the time. Nothing domestic in it, for sure.

Magnificent day. The storm last night cleared the air, the sky blue, washed and all things resting in the sudden coolness. Cooking. Everything fresh, the color of the eggplants dark purple, glossy, the capsicums. I felt slightly guilty cutting all those vital tissues. What if they had some feeling in them?

Watering the garden, the perfume of the water falling on the heated leaves, the heated ground, sizzling, the horizon blue clear. Holiday weather.

JOURNAL V

OUTBACK

JULY

We left at 5 a.m. Everyone in a good mood. We traveled out of the city. Snow at Katoomba, snowmen in gardens, slosh on the highway. Snowing heavily at Lithgow. Very beautiful landscape as in Romania, we took photos, these amazing picturesque frames, the trees, the fields all white, small houses in the distance, the snow falling in drifts across the windows.

Very cold. We stopped for lunch in Orange. New coffee shop in what used to be the Canobolas Saloon Bar.

We reached Dubbo by late afternoon and drove to Kathy and Gabriel's. All very pleased to see us. Dioni and Marina older now, showing us their schoolbooks. Both very pretty, with short hair, serious eyes, already considering fundamental questions of existence.

Gabriel had cooked us his Borlotos Granados soup, with borlotti beans, pumpkin, sweet corn, onion and tomato.

Not his mythical soup that Jolanta and Jurgis kept telling me about, the so-called *Curanto* prepared on Dangar Island, in some historic time, when I was not present. A soup made with pork, chicken, mussels, crab, prawns, fish, potatoes, onions, Spanish sausages, cumin, chilli . . . and so on. A soup made for sterner stomachs, outside my range.

WILCANNIA

A deserted, dusty, forsaken place. Empty streets, closed shops with planked-up windows, peeling. An Aboriginal man leaning against the door of the old pub. Seen through the veranda post he looked out of a Drysdale painting, his body leaning forward. He was thin, with white hair, but not that old, his hat over his forehead, dressed in a neat gray jacket.

In the center, Major Mitchell's bronze statue, half-size, a midget, pointing in some large gesture toward the empty street and the petrol station.

Then on the road to Broken Hill. On and on, flat, open horizons, the landscape gray-silver, the earth ochre-red, large trucks, dead kangaroos in the emptiness that went for miles.

Cozy in the car, the motor humming. Country-style music with an easy beat on the radio, and an advertisement for "Chicken à la Russe"—at Papa Joe's.

At dusk we stopped at this pub stranded in the emptiness. The publican and his wife very friendly. As we were leaving three tall young men, in dungarees, with dusty faces came in, laughing, as if from a field of adventure.

"Where have you come from?" we asked.

And they: "Drilling in the paddocks."

They seemed full of energy and spirit. We drove toward Broken Hill in a good mood too. The moon up, kangaroos crossing the road from time to time, one stopping in front of the car as we slowed down, then making a dash for it to the other side.

BROKEN HILL

A large country town with substantial, handsome buildings in light stone. I had imagined it full of black soot, dust, but in fact very clean, everything polished for its new image as a historic town.

Mario's Palace Hotel, a very imposing nineteenth-century building with massive balconies in wrought iron, verandas all around, built by a Frenchman in the 1840s. Inside, the Signora, a tall, elegant woman with delicate features, was sitting at a desk in a room with very high, ornate ceilings, surrounded by carved birds, stuffed birds, totems, pieces of galena, rocks of silver, a dusted magnificence, a baroque accumulation of paraphernalia. I became very enthusiastic, asked permission to take photos, she became enthusiastic with my enthusiasm.

Going to our rooms, up the circular cedar staircase, the walls full of murals, the work of an Aboriginal artist, Gordon White, who, when coming to town, paints a mural in exchange for his board. Outback landscapes, horsemen riding in dark-blue hills. And on the ceiling, above the staircase, Mario's full-blown copy of Botticelli's *The Birth of Venus* in a glory of color.

We ate at the renamed Socialist Democratic Club, before it was the Socialist Club. The place full, poker machines, paintings on the walls by local artists, and people eating T-bone steaks and chips.

Broken Hill full of artists and art galleries. Everyone telling us to visit Pro Hart's. But the ex-miner in charge of the Mineral Museum urged us to go and see Hugh Schultz's studio, just around the corner.

We went through an open garage and knocked at the back door. Schultz, a tall, white-haired man with warm, laughing eyes, a ready wit, full of stories about his life, kids, paintings, adventures, prospecting, gambling, loose women, drink. An accident at the mine turned him to painting.

His paintings full of light, a feeling that the red fields are flying too with his birds and his flowers. He took us to meet his wife and her sister, who were watching television in the lounge room. As we were leaving, he was accompanying us with yet another story about black panthers in the hills and Sergeant McLaughlan.

His landscapes stayed with you, light, transparent whites, luminous pinks, reds, birds everywhere flying, they seemed the spirit of the land.

SILVERTON

Marvelous white gums by the creek. Camels on the way, by the roadside, eating grass, gum leaves.

Silverton, once a busy mining town with nearly three thousand people in 1885, slowly deserted as fresh fields of lead, silver, zinc were discovered in Broken Hill.

Up on the hill bitterly cold and windy, ruins of houses, closed churches, the small museum. Tourists riding camels as in a Nolan painting.

We had a drink at the famous Silverton Hotel. From the veranda, the hills as in Greece, human, a gray apricot tinge to them. Saltbushes, silvery gray clumps, the ground a warm yellow red. On the horizon, an undulating line of hills called *The Monks*.

TIBOOBURRA

We drove all day to Tibooburra on dirt roads, rough, hard ground. Semidesert country, red ochre, amazing hill formations, little or nothing on the horizon, another valley over the small hills. A dispirited fox was crossing the road at Fowler's Gap, head down, burdened with worries.

We reached Tibooburra by mid-afternoon. We booked at the Family Hotel, Clifton Pugh's place. But Jurgis was very keen to see the Dingo Fence, the mythological creature he had heard so much about. So we left again, driving through the Sturt National Park. It was getting dark, we passed an immense clay pan, the wind icy, the colors muddy, quite a sinister feeling to it.

Then on and on, faster over a hill, then another, soft undulating country, Jurgis saying that the whole continent has these hills, a friend traveled across them up to Western Australia. We passed the Ranger's House, Fort Gray, the distance never-ending, all of us silently uneasy of finding our way back in the dark.

Finally, we arrived at Cameron's Corner, named after the surveyor John Cameron, who completed the first boundary survey between NSW and Queensland in 1882. And the Dingo Fence. Nothing spectacular, just an ordinary high wire fence, and the white post marking the boundaries of the three States—NSW, Qld and SA.

The sun already down as we turned back, no cars anywhere, the bush silver gray in the moonlight. Kangaroos waiting elegantly in the evening silence, this marvelous echidna, its delicate bone needles moving up and down, frantically trying to dig itself into the ground, while we took photos.

To our great relief we arrived back in Tibooburra. The Family Hotel looked like an old country house, solid sandstone walls, large verandas. The locals were drinking in what must have been the original front room of the house, high ceilings, a fire going on, loud music, tall, thin men reached the height of the bar, and on the wall, Pugh's rather lurid pictures of naked women.

We went into the dining room, empty now, later two men came in with beers in their hands, walking carefully on their rubber legs.

But our rooms at the back were additions made of fibro, the summer dust still on everything.

I had fallen asleep, when suddenly, under my window, this loud transistor was wailing in the night, then drunken voices responding, shouts, coming in waves through the window, the tin walls . . . disappearing around the corner, coming back again.

In the next room, two men came in, their voices gurgling with some undefined sound in their mouths . . . they fell into bed with a thud and were gone, no sound out of them, like birds asleep.

But the woman with the transistor—Michelle, we learned in the morning—kept putting the sound higher and higher, as she came into her room the whole place shook with the beat of some country singer's voice. She was singing with it, a young voice, monotonous, disjointed, stubborn, and all of us, in our beds listening. The bush outside silent, spacious, full of marvelously delicate colors, washed silver grays, red ochres with yellow tinges, the large boulders at the edge of town marking an Aboriginal sacred site.

Jurgis knocked on her door after 1 a.m. She turned the transistor off, but her voice went on in the night, mournful, chanting, sending a challenge to the night, some deep complaint, using the same song, on and on, breaking it, rising with it toward some escape.

We fell in and out of sleep, trapped in the place, in the middle of the country that was silent under the moonlight, mysterious, singing out of some deep sorrow, some terrible loss . . .

Over breakfast, we all thought that Tibooburra must be Tourmaline in Randolph Stow's book. In the daytime, the place quite friendly, the houses in washed-out colors, dusty and in the card shop behind the counter, a couple coming out of an Arbus photograph.

We drove out. Stopped for lunch in the middle of a field of yellow daisies. The billy boiling, the sun quite warm. This land, living very well without us, and we just passing visitors, as Pasternak said.

We arrived back in Broken Hill at dusk. On the way kangaroos by the roadside, mother and child, standing upright, dignified and at ease, watching the sunset and us, the barbarians, approaching and disappearing in a cloud of dust.

Rabbits crossing the road, in a hurry. Emus. But the sheep, heavy, like some artificial creatures invented by someone without an aesthetic sense, crossing the road with their heavy backsides.

At night, we had fish at the Pussy Cat Café, came back through the deserted streets, at the back of the hotel, the massive black hill of tailings.

MENINDEE

On the way, saltbushes, desert apples, the grave of Dost Mahomet, part of the Burke and Wills expedition of 1860–62.

Tea by the banks of the lake, large old gum trees, flaking, the ground full of debris, the water sparkling in the sun, the weir. The large boiler of the paddle-steamer *Providence*, which blew up in 1872, killing all the crew. Their graves in the Kinchega National Park. Their names not known.

At the Menindee Hotel everything in order. The new owners from Petersham in Sydney. An interior courtyard, large verandas, the room where Burke stayed in 1860, before the tragic journey.

In the printed manifesto they gave us, describing the history of the town and the hotel, previously Maiden's Menindee Hotel, we are told: "These walls are witnesses to real Australian history."

After dinner we went for a walk down the main street. Darkness, emptiness, a few lighted houses, a car passing at speed, dogs barking. The stars and the moon out.

As we passed the Menindee Café with its large glass front, and the blue painted door, we looked inside. An elderly woman dressed totally in black, with a black kerchief over her hair, was sitting at one of the small tables.

She looked like the wife in Angelopoulos's film *Journey to Kythera*—some mute acceptance of what life brings, one imagined that if we went in, she would ask immediately if we had eaten, bring food to the table.

Her lonely image in the night, in that abandoned street, in the middle of nowhere, enormously sad, touching. The Greeks, always on the move, struggling with their fish and chips, holding on to their mothers dressed in black.

Our last day. We left early, drove toward the Flinders Ranges. Beautiful morning, sunny, warm. We stopped on top of a ridge. Jolanta and Jurgis sketching. A large lizard on a rock pretending to be dead, not moving at all, not even its eyelids. When it heard the click of my camera, it attacked, opening its pink mouth, a hissing sound, rather feebly.

The ground full of mica and quartz, white transparent and light pink stones. We drove further in, between the hills, had lunch. Talked of poetry, the past again, the war, refugees, hundreds of us on the move across Europe, ending in places we had hardly heard of, in those summers, a long time ago in Braila, Mother talking of Stendhal and *Le Rouge et le Noir*, nothing at that time pointing to any moves, any changes in the landscape of our lives.

Suddenly, from the corner of my eye, between the car and the saltbushes, a curious group of young emus was advancing silently, floating on the landscape, casing us as if some interesting animals, lowering their heads to have a better view, walking toward us, but not quite near enough. We took photos. Spoke to them. When Jolanta got up to get her sketchbook, they became frightened, and scuttled away on the wind, stopped from afar to look at us, elegantly bending their heads to pick up some food, watch some more.

We came back into Broken Hill, high on the light, the hills, and the emus—the loveliness of their presence.

JOURNAL VI

JANUARY

With Beth at the Sydney Town Hall for the Suzuki concert. Children and music and the Town Hall looking very beautiful now after the renovations. I remembered all the concerts I heard there, at the beginning, when listening to real music was a necessity, now all replaced with mechanical voices.

The presence of musicians and instruments on stage, all these young girls playing harps, the instruments like a series of mechanized dolls, remembered Fellini and his Orchestral Rehearsal—the musicians discussing their instruments as if intimate friends with personalities.

A young woman playing the Sibelius violin concerto, the first part only. Well sustained, good phrasing, warm tone that went well with the somberness, the sadness of the music. Who was she? Young, good-looking, in an amazing red tulle dress with sparkles, totally at odds with the music.

Then the younger ones at the piano. I was telling Beth of my beginnings at home with Madame Papanti, her tall, thin, bony figure going down the corridor of the small music school, telling me not to look at the keys while I was playing.

Isabel Allende speaking of the worldview of Latin American Indians who believe that one's past is before one, providing knowledge for the acquisition of wisdom, while the future is just a black pit behind.

Jean Genet was being interviewed by the BBC. This baby-faced, mild-looking individual. The interviewer not very good, constantly interrupting the flow of the responses and trying to pin him down to his homosexuality, homosexuality as politics. Genet laughed ironically, a contempt over his face about this lack of understanding.

Why was he living in Morocco?

Why shouldn't he live in Morocco?

How did he spend his days?

Genet smiled inwardly. "You mean . . . the question of time? I shall reply with St. Augustine's line: I am waiting for death."

His life so terrible, partly self-made, the constant movement between prisons, army, churches, most of the places that he had been in were one or the other, army camps transformed into schools for delinquents, monasteries turned into prisons and so on.

His vocabulary full of the resonances of these three powers. A precise use of language, awareness of it, sharp intellectual analysis of life, sadness, but at the same time, this "oblique angle," as he called it, and with it a total contempt for any value, the terrible places he had been in, his view of people, of life, not only through gay eyes, but constantly despising the rest of the world which is not like him.

Hating the French and French civilization, yet totally shaped by it, quite exhilarating to hear his attitude to language use, the past, literature.

Full of contempt for the 1968 student revolution in France. He was in the National Theater when it happened. Revolutionaries should take over the Police Headquarters, the Law Courts, the church, not the National Theatre. The discussions and the speeches in the takeover were just as in his bordello plays, a circular movement, from the floor to the stage and back again, never going out, but kept internally.

FEBRUARY

Xenakis on the radio. A piece called *Bohor No 1.* Pure sounds, linear music, like a very tight, abstract pale light, the essence of the human voice, sounds of streets erupting as in a demonstration, the bells tolling, on and on, as with crowds in a series of waves, resonances of large railway stations, shootings, then stopping abruptly.

Raining again, but not in the country where needed. At night these explosions of white spectral light, waiting for the thunder that seemed to take a long time in coming, and when it finally did, as if from far away, while the lightning, bombs of light landing in my room, on my closed eyelids . . .

I was thinking last night that out of the boredom of these everydays, that we feel bring nothing, watching only a few dogs walking aimlessly down the street, the papers pushed by the wind, the milky light falling on the houses, out of this time kneads unheard, the next happenings of one's life and suddenly they hit you, imperceptibly at first as always, but later holding on to you with a savage persistence.

Kids growing, walking in the street, watching the air, the houses, the dogs with interest. The adventure has begun. Barbara's little boy, Harry, born last year, he is already holding himself totally erect, tackling the street, running after their dog. The everyday miraculous.

MARCH

Last night on the TV the work of the Czech animator Jan Svankmajer. A savage vision of the world, of people. People eating each other, spitting each other out, all these busts made of clay, coming together in passion, then demolishing each other.

The figures earthbound, chilly and heavy-looking, the actual melting of their lips, eyes, hands, heads in these bursts of manic anger.

A razor-edged vision.

In the magazine, an article on the work of artists in mental institutions, very colorful, fantastic.

Dubuffet collected them and then donated them to the city of Lausanne. Dubuffet summing up the collections: "There is no art of the insane any more than there is an art of dyspeptics or an art of people with knee complaints.

"These works may often be rudimentary . . . but they are charged, perhaps more strongly than the works of celebrated artists, with everything that can be asked of a work of art: burning mental tension, uncurbed invention, an ecstasy of intoxication, complete liberty. Mad? Of Course. Can you conceive of an art which is not mad?"

Mitchell Galleries spacious, with high ceilings and a noble line. I was there to hear the Canadian writer. The writer, modest and at ease. Tales of his readings in remote schools, reluctant audiences, or readings as Szymborska's poem has put it: "three members of the family and two out of the rain . . ."

He read a long story about an earthquake he experienced when he was eight. I remembered the one I had experienced at about the same age.

At night. What I remembered was not the movement of the furniture, or of the people, but the noise, the terrifying noise together with a total shaking, the walls that seemed to touch each other, the deep groans, as if the earth was telling us of her deep sorrow, the flashes of blue light and then Father searching frantically for us, calling us.

When we finally came out of the house, the trees were swaying with this terrifying noise and from what seemed the pores, the cracks in the ground, these small, blue flames were sprouting, together with the sound, like heaving, as if the joints of the world, these gigantic joints, were turning, readjusting . . .

Tosti on the radio, and Tino Rossi. This music in which we all flow, the dead, the living, the future. Father used to sing him at home, and Mother would tease him about his voice.

She was talking to me on the phone about him. He had gone. He was not coming back. He was preoccupied with his inner problems, unsolvable, constant, totally self-absorbing. Evaluations, which in spite of his seeming generosity admitted no one, became destructive, childish in their demands, rising out of the circumstances of his life toward some desired state, which was somewhere else, that constantly promised to be achieved.

APRIL

Renato Amato it seemed had died at thirty-five. Sneja published him in her book *Displacements: Migrant Story-Tellers.*

I always remembered the evening at his house, a long time ago. A sort of state of siege, energy that was being squandered on everyone, like someone killing and spluttering blood all around in an effort to engage them all, when everyone refused to be engaged, the whole country, in fact, refused to respond.

The house, one of those small, wooden houses, mock modern, with narrow corridors, passages that led to bedrooms where children were asleep. His wife, a blonde, silent girl, looked as if someone living permanently in pain, and he kept hacking away at the air, the enemies all invisible and never rising to the challenge.

I remember that he kept saying how low he had sunk—"he was a public servant now." He spat the words out as if obscenities, a thing that he looked on with contempt, in Italy.

In Canberra to visit Kazys, see some exhibitions and look for mushrooms. The mist rising over the hills, the unfolding layers of forest. We went into a clearing, a park by the little river, beautiful European trees, an alley with their dark-gray trunks, the top branches as if full of snow. Birch trees, on the ground their small leaves, deep brown, ochre white and bright dark yellow. Further down, a large group of poplars turning golden, enclosing between them a space, a mystery, the silence.

In the forest, the light coming through the green leaves, suddenly a field of mushrooms, mushrooms everywhere, everyone very enthusiastic, rushing to collect better ones, the buzzing of flies from time to time, and far up, the mournful, broken, lamenting sound of currawongs.

We had billy tea in the clearing, sat on logs, discussed, far above, the trees in the sun, no sound at all. And then it started, the wind, the slight hum at the crest of the trees. One forgets how beautiful nature is! Trees! Trees! One should write a rhapsody to trees.

Vassy's voice on the phone was empty, as if drained, washed out. She wasn't crying, Nutzy had died, on Thursday, she went very quickly, in five minutes, they were all there by her bedside. She had asked the sister: "Sister, am I dying?"

And the sister had answered: "What do you think?"

And Nutzy had said: "I am dying." And she was gone in a few minutes. Marully and all of them devastated by her death. How could it have happened?

I was thinking of her all this week. Orphaned, living with her father that she resembled, a soft-spoken, handsome-looking man.

Nutzy seemed to have taken from him this soft way of speaking, an attachment to beautiful things, yet at the same time, she had a sharp, biting wit.

Anzac Day. In the kitchen, looking at the whitish light, the empty day, all this death and heroism on the radio, on television. Elderly men and women with white hair singing, priests and politicians talking of patriotism. The dead, as usual, underground and silent. What were they thinking of? That countries should always define themselves by war?

MAY

Beautiful, still, autumn weather. Looking through old papers trying to find a line: "we must sink into the fragility of the moment as if we know of no other eternity . . ."

The delicate, dry leg of a cockroach among the papers. Trying to work on the conference paper, on and on, so much work on it and still not finished. Texts—like giant beasts always out of control, enlarging here and there, shrinking here and there, constantly needing attention.

A documentary on Cocteau. He was telling us: "A writer ought to be a serious person who adopts an air of frivolity out of politeness."

This beautiful blue-black-coated bird with a white waistcoat landed on the letterbox. Its tail trailing along and in constant movement, opening and closing like a fan, the movement of Spanish dancers, abrupt but very graceful. Then it jumped on the grass to attack some food.

Near the mandarin tree Max asleep, stretching with enormous pleasure, his whiskers glinting in the sun, at his back, a pigeon knocking the grass.

• • •

Listening to Marie Claire Allain last night playing this ferocious-looking organ, what a terrible instrument, terrible in the biblical sense, inhuman somehow, the product of a Nordic imagination, out of proportion with the human. I have never taken to it, totally outside my musical background.

But still, coming into Notre Dame, that late afternoon during Holy Week, the place crowded with people, yet looking spacious and elegant, and Bach's Toccata sounding apocalyptical from the high arches, the sound was awesome. It has remained in me as a magnificent experience.

Claire Allain played some very moving pieces by Bach, a hymn—"I call unto thee Jesus." She kept saying how human Bach was, how lyrical, rising toward the infinite, so high one could hardly follow him. This tendency to rise upward and out of ourselves, difficult to find means of expressing it.

JUNE

Finally on our way to Lake Mungo. We traveled via Hay. The sunset before Hay spectacular, flat, open plains advancing into this sea of colors, overwhelming. Deep reds, golden yellows, blue pinks. We watched them avidly. Took photos.

Driving the whole of next day. The same round, flat horizons stretching for miles, the infatuation of space. Dark saltbushes and the kangaroos on the way, dark too like the scrub.

We reached Mungo late afternoon. No one around. We looked at the displays in the little museum. The history of the place from ancient times, Aboriginal remains, artifacts. The Mungo Lady, 25,000 years, 35,000 years, dates to give one vertigo. Finally we found the Shearers Huts where we were going to spend the night. Corrugated iron cabins with beds.

The emptiness of the place. Above the giant dry lake full of black saltbushes, the sky was opalescent gray-pink. The woolshed a dusted presence. I stayed outside moved by the subtle luminosity that enveloped everything. From the lighted kitchen, Jurgis's and Jolanta's voices could be heard talking with Richard, the only traveler we had found there.

In the big dining room the walls painted with prehistoric giant animals, we ate mashed potatoes and chops, in line with what the shearers would have had.

At midnight, the sky very low and dense with stars. The Milky Way lighted up with a thousand light bulbs, crystal points sparkling in the darkness. Everything low, the whole panoply, and very brilliant. I kept turning round and round below this fantastic ceiling sparkling in the night.

Later the wind started, a surreptitious, slightly sinister wind, moving as if tresses of hair on the sand, advancing in silence, retreating. Then the rain, the sky covered in clouds and all the brilliance of the stars gone, a whitish gauze over the ceiling of the sky.

In the morning we walked up to the Walls of China, from the distance looking massive, as if carved in sandstone. Freezing cold. The wind blowing and a light rain coming down. We walked into this lunar landscape, small plants, stunted trees growing at the base of the sandhills.

Silence, the most fundamental substance of the place. The wind moving through the bushes, then the sound of running water, as I was standing halfway up a hill. I looked around to see where the sound of water could have come from, realized that it was the wind moving through the saltbushes.

We had to leave as the rain began to fall heavily, the roads unsealed, paprika-red ground everywhere and beautiful blond porcupine grass.

JULY

A French program on the TV on Albert Einstein. One begins to be more aware of the magnificence of the universe, physics, mathematics. The continuous wonder of it all. I remembered at school in Greece when I began to do physics in earnest with Mrs. Theano, how enthusiastic I was, giving Mother all this information on our walks by the sea in Lavrion.

The program full of insights, too fast to remember any, but one which I liked. Einstein saying: "The real is so subtle."

He was discussing the fugitive, relative nature of things, seeing stars that have disappeared, whose light still traveled. He checked his theory of relativity by photographing a total eclipse. Einstein was full of admiration for the perfection of the curve of light around the dark sun. They asked him what he would have done if the light did not show a perfect curve, and he said, he would have assumed that God was absent-minded, and had forgotten to utilise a perfectly good theory, and he would have reprimanded Him severely.

• • •

Chagall's graphics in the white, clean gallery. His etchings marvelously young, enormous feeling of lightness about them, the blues, the greens, the reds, and that light line. A touch to the left and they would have become sentimental, a touch to the right and they would have become heavy, but he maintained his balance very well.

Cold and overcast, the garden naked. The new dog next door waits, bored with his loneliness and the day. Max, sitting near the gate eyes him continuously, this invasion of dogs everywhere has him in a permanent state of despondency.

He walks toward the gate, his eye on the dog, and wails angrily in a low, monotonous key.

At Angela's. We ate in the garden, sunny, overlooking Coogee, the cemetery. They were barbecuing further down, someone was calling out: "Milos . . . Milos . . ."

Ileana was playing with the kids next door. They fell in together immediately. In the car back, she was showing me her book of stick-ons—animals, flowers, people. She looked very lovely, a milky skin and her blue eyes with long eyelashes, everything new, vulnerable. This miracle that always catches one by surprise.

A documentary about a Chinese woman artist in the USA—Kam. She was talking about Chinese arts, methods, calligraphy, the symbols, the brushstrokes, the landscape, the inversion of perspective, the actual brushes, implements, jars, beautiful to look at, the caring approach to one's tools.

The lotus rising out of the mud, this beautiful flower opens the first day and closes the first night, opens the second day, and closes the second night, and then remains open . . . Something in its hesitancy.

Proverbs such as: A pretty girl is an accident of nature, but a beautiful woman is a creation from inside.

They filmed her hand in the process of doing calligraphy, as if a bird in flight over the white paper.

AUGUST

Marvelous days, warm, sunny, the apricot has already began to blossom, in such a hurry, as if the weather spurs it on.

The delicate transparent pink petals like folded minuscule fans, the currawongs were eating them the day before, making those long sounds, like resonant spears they were sending into the sky. Jet black with white under their tails, and their eyes a round circle of tinselled gold.

Lunch in the garden under the trees at Nadine's, the white-haired painter was sitting next to me, his very naive blue eyes were full of warmth.

We gave him a lift as we left, stopped for a while at the wharf to have a look at Sydney, at night, the spectacular view of the outline of the lighted city, the ferries crossing and the dark sea moving below as if a live, heavy element. Pinchgut like a face with two eyes looking wistfully at something.

Then James remembered the story of the lighthouse and the foghorn. The lighthouse keeper woken suddenly in the middle of the night by a cry, a howling. When he came out the mist was everywhere and out of the mist this monster rose to reply to the foghorn with which he had fallen in love.

He was making these howling love cries, to finally embrace it and drag it down to the depths of the sea.

Littlemore on the ABC's Media Watch, quoting from the Western Courier. A local man applying to the Council.

The paper described him as: "a Korean from Doonside."

I was laughing at the combination.

"An Australian," said Littlemore, darkly, before vanishing from the screen, with a glint in his eyes, behind his glasses.

What is surprising about prejudice is how it operates without any direction, in an open society, free speech and all that, but underneath it all, everyone is programmed and the attitudes operate as efficiently as if in the army.

Almost the beginning of spring. The small lizards are coming out, running across the path.

Two bulbuls bathing in the water dish, splashing about, shaking their wings, their tails, the water drops breaking in the light, a luminous web around them.

Three sparrows are waiting for their turn, as if at a public bath. Later a slight wind blowing, a nervous sparrow drinking rapidly and listening to the sound.

SEPTEMBER

Jurgis's exhibition. His Birds of Paradise looking magnificent at the entry of the gallery. He catches the everydayness of life in Australia that somehow few painters attempt. The suburbs. The painting of the Hume Highway, which I liked very much, with a large blue truck, the corner shop in the rain, the silvery-gray liquid sky and the pavements—full of lightness.

Watching last night on Compass this very good film about the last Yahi, called Ishi. The Yahis, an Indian tribe in America, were decimated by the whites, cleaning up the continent.

He lived with his companions for forty years, then they were starving. In one of the last raids the whites took their blankets. He could not survive the cold, so he walked out into what was now white territory.

Anthropologists immediately at work, his language that no one understood . . .

This very gentle, polite, civilized person in touch with deeper forces, mythologies, professions, in the European sense, with his hunting, his tool making, beautiful arrows, arrowheads. An all-rounded person that the newspapers constantly described as The Last Savage.

He was telling the anthropologists their histories, the creation of the world, the going of the dead, looking for the opening to the underworld, leaving one by one, searching for the entrance, in the ground, in the sky.

In the photographs, which they constantly took of him, he was looking at them, at the world, with very sad, human eyes.

He died of tuberculosis. He was telling one of the anthropologists that had become his friend, that he will wait for him on the other side.

The sudden heat, the air free somehow and light, the powerful scent of jasmine in the house, the open doors, windows, make one suddenly aware of oneself, one's life, sadness.

Barenboim playing a Beethoven sonata on the radio, suddenly the old poem alive:

Drunk
on honeysuckle scent
and moonlight
the memory of your eyes . . .

Traveling to the reading. The night very warm, blue, the lights everywhere.

The hotel, an impersonal place, pink walls, lots of aluminum and moving staircases. Along corridors, past reception rooms that were being arranged in the new style of what is assumed is an easy elegance, a hard combination made to appeal to businessmen, the new military class of the world with their stiff rituals. The tables were being arranged with red tablecloths, glass holders with peanuts and chips and lots of serviettes.

The room where we were going to read in pink too, with a black rostrum, small ceiling lights, but when the rostrum lights came on, the light shone straight into your eyes.

We waited a long time for people to turn up. Finally some fifty were there, friends of the readers, other writers. The young man reading before me had a rough voice, a de rigueur voice developed in pubs, which they are giving us in literature too and think that this makes them Australian. A sort of inner brutality now that masks pretentiousness, an energy that never questions itself, a battering of language with no sense of its fragility, the beautiful energy, the dynamics that can be released when well used.

When I came to the platform after the introduction I was already angry. Why was I there? What did I have in common with these people? The darkness beyond the black, metal podium seemed like an empty, heavy space.

One could see nothing in the distance beyond the strong lights but some empty chairs. Where were they? What were they thinking?

Only the immense silence of their listening came forward and I with myself. I began to read without any feeling for the poems, just to get over the reading. I read fast, feeling the emptiness, the darkness and the silence as an immense weight that had to be activated, a neutral sea that dragged everything down, so that the spaces between the words seemed enormous and I felt that they had to be filled in.

We went with Patricia to look for a flat for her while she would be in Sydney performing.

The Paradise Lodge did not seem too bad from outside. But inside, these long, dark corridors, with small lights and the rooms in dark concrete. As if people that had lived there had left nothing behind them, as if the material used did not allow for any accumulation, change, humanization.

A material that constantly rejected every approach, human-proof, that was concerned only with maintaining its icy temperature and not cracking too early. The black vinyl, the concrete-sprayed walls, the mock wooden texture, a material with no base in itself, no core, just thin layers, an amalgam of unmatched materials forced to stay together by technology.

The materials not very happy about it, staying together for the minimum of time and then disassociating themselves from each other, breaking, turning away, flaking.

OCTOBER

The weather the whole weekend beautiful, a perfection that kept you going out, looking at the sky, a deep, perfect blueness, the view over the city, the trees, everyone out cleaning, pruning, rearranging, as if we all wanted to look good for the newly arrived visitor.

At the Bondi Pavilion for the exhibition. Bondi at night looking quite ethereal. Early evening, the light still on the sea and the houses, the shops on the other side lit up, the Bondi Hotel—a large cake full of lights, festive.

A documentary on Berkoff. Uneasy, clever, very good mimic, violent, quite handsome, rather repetitive view of things as if constantly hitting this metal plate of violence, not much resonance to it or nuances.

He was saying that during the war he was evacuated from London. A pupil in a small school in the country where he heard constantly how the Jews had killed Christ. He felt terrible, he imagined that some of his distant relatives must have been involved.

In the afternoon we had coffee. Everything in the house rested. Then toward five a big wind came up, the temperature dropped suddenly with amazing rapidity, the city covered in dust, the trees bending, the houses creaking, dead leaves everywhere, birds flying low, twisted suddenly in the current.

Later the wind died down, a green moon came up, icy green with a transparent circle around it, vaguely sketched. At Harold Park the races were on.

Dinner at Pat's. The day very hot, forty-three degrees, a heavy stilted light over the city. The sky pouring this invisible melting heat over you, the stillness absolute as if the city was empty. Finally, late afternoon the cool change came.

Discussions around the table. Gwyneth. Always her warm, generous presence, talking of films, books, reading *The Empress Wu* by Fitzgerald.

Adrian on his favorite topic, journalism and newspapers, the typesetters, the printing staff, all gone now. No one on the premises any longer, the journalists writing from home, unrelated to each other, sending the material in, the papers printed by large machines controlled by a few mechanics.

The demise of the afternoon papers, he felt they reflected an Australian reality, a gutsy roughness, not these niceties that the morning papers were constantly pretending to, their boring respectability.

When we left the night had turned wild, the temperature had dropped and the wind blew the trees, moved the lanterns, the chimes in the garden.

Patrick White's voice on the radio talking of Australian Literature and how it can be developed only from inner experiences, when there are people making inner discoveries in this landscape, and have the courage to write about them.

NOVEMBER

Thinking of the film about Anaïs Nin and Henry Miller by Kaufman. The image emerging from the film of two poseurs, incapable of involvement, pushing the sexual to its limits but in a saccharine way, an amazing coyness both in tone and in details, in spite of the sex scenes, heavy breathing, women as if dolls, photographed in glow colors, naked, then perfectly dressed, almost clinical in their dress perfection.

An American time in Europe in the thirties, grandiose ideas of conquering Europe, a sort of American ockerism. Miller surviving on American energy, a boyish, pamphleteering sort of energy.

Even his essays, which I liked, more enthusiasm than observation, over-excitement, and pleased with his over-excitement. Being sure that this is what liberation is, freedom, yet at the same time unable to let go, tight inwardly and very Calvinistic in spite of all the sexual excesses. A person uneasy everywhere, constantly trying brutally to break all conventions in the hope that it will bring him inner freedom.

Alexandra came for afternoon coffee bringing a book to show me: *Private Lives* by Mark Bryant, *A True Compendium of Curious Facts, Bizarre Habits, and Fascinating Anecdotes About the Private Lives of the Famous and Infamous Throughout History*. Under Rabelais—his will is supposed to have contained the following: "I owe much. I possess nothing. I give the rest to the poor."

On television, a film of Pirandello's *Henry IV*, Mastroianni in the title role and Claudia Cardinale, her daughter also, looking remarkably like her when young.

Very well played. Pirandello always manages to say something of substance. This man that is or pretends to be Henry IV. The power of obsessions over other people, someone who totally underscores all the rational evaluations of life, who builds another base and proceeds to live accordingly, throwing everyone else into chaos. The man seems to suffer from an emotional disappointment, a refusal to accept things as they are, a contempt for what life offers, a contempt for himself ultimately, yet has an enormous self-assurance that things are as he sees them.

A subtle portrait of a dictator.

DECEMBER

It was a marvelous night, a slight breeze, warm with a full moon. After dinner we talked in the dark, came out on the terrace to watch the moon, splendid over the city.

It was a night like those in my childhood, far away, the star slightly below the moon, and in the distance the buildings burning with a crisp light.

The night full of peace.

Nikos came from Melbourne for the opening of his exhibition. He was calling from the garden with his flowers, these exotic lilies that looked as if made of wax.

He was very nervous, as always, before an opening. We drove to the gallery early, the space good and the paintings hung well. The large individual flowers glowing with rich colors, reds of the most amazing quality, as if they included every imaginable color—yellows, dark greens—beautiful presences.

The orchids, large and ferocious-looking, taking up the whole canvas, looking like New Guinean masked dancers, full of menace, darkness, uncertainty. He saw them as sexual, transformed them into symbols of fecundity, pods of heavy seed, yet so centrally placed that they became a symbol for people, plants, some sexual universality.

One felt that he had reached a totally personal style, a mastery of color, at close range, the strokes seemed to carry the essential force of the paintings.

We were swimming, floating in this sea of colors, elated.

Traveling to the Arts and Crafts Exhibition. Sunday afternoon, the whole day the wind blew and the sky dusty, mustard almost, from the bushfires. The sun, a small pink circle at the bottom of the sky. The light outside as if dipped in lime, a white blue phosphorescence. Inside the house, when it fell on white, it was orange, gold apricot. In the bathroom it glinted golden on the blue tiles. I could not have enough of it. I kept looking outside, waiting for the taxi, the leaves fanned constantly in this phosphorescent white light.

The exhibition in the Greek church, a hall at the back. A newly built church, a heavy model of modest churches in small towns. Everything about it new, wide steps, windswept. In the afternoon apocalyptic light, the small, black-dressed women, blown by the wind, going upward on the steps, disappearing inside.

The exhibits—delicate embroideries of past centuries, deep reds with silver and gold threads, as if embossed. Church chalises, vestments, household items. Mr. Evanghelatos came to greet me, how kind of me to come. The angle of his shoulders cloaked in humility.

Reading a biography of Georgia O'Keeffe by Laurie Lisle:

> The unleashed forces of nature seemed to meet and free some similar emotional energy in Georgia, instead

of intimidating her, their wildness and unpredictability made her euphoric and repeatedly she enthusiastically described them as—"beautiful."

. . . for the rest of her life she would speak of the plains as her spiritual home, "that was my country, terrible wind and a wonderful emptiness."

She had plans to be reincarnated in her next life as a blonde with a beautiful, soprano voice.

"I would sing very high, very clear notes," she said, "without fear."

JOURNAL VII

JANUARY

One hundred fires raging over hundreds of kilometers since December, the black burnt leaves arriving here too, in the garden, black soot in the house, everywhere. An acrid smell of smoke in the house, the sun totally red, a little red dot in the milky sky. Everyone tired, the firefighters above all, people in the mountains with their bags packed, just in case.

The whole city covered in smoke, one can't see beyond the bridge. We are ringing friends to see that they are all right.

Thinking last night of all the people that have gone. And the future? Mysteries everywhere and fear, the two major ingredients. Eleni ringing from Athens to wish me a good year. The things we are saying every year without knowing what the next day will bring.

In the dream I was at a table with people eating pastries, in this desert area, arid, small saltbushes, the ground full of broken stones, pebbles, warm, ochre colors.

Then suddenly in this emptiness, on the line of the horizon a large pool, as if a small, round lake, all filled with blood. The surface of the lake still, the blood deep red surrounded by sand-colored scrub.

A documentary on Lena Horne. The amazing changes in her dramatically beautiful face. Coming back to performing after the McCarthy era, in which she lost all her contracts, went through the anti-American Committee. Young, in her forties probably, but her face, a devastated face, showing all the terrible events she had been through, petrified somehow in this wounded person. I had never seen this in such a stark way, a point inside her that weighed everything down.

Dinner at Anna and Hilik's. The house full of Hilik's sculptures, catching you from all angles, the walls, the ceiling, the tops of tables, under the tables, the staircase. His use of wood very good, shapes everywhere that are alive, that speak, that work within their forms, like a forest of beings.

Good food as always, fresh salads, prawns, mussels in their brown-green shells, translucent white fish, luminous like Anna's style.

Around the table a friendly group of people, a young painter, who blushed almost every time he looked at his partner, an English beauty, tall, cool, with a raucous laughter in between long silences. She had worked with cosmetics, and now was working with crystals, the magic potential of crystals.

It finally rained the night before, a relief, the fires in the mountains put out, but on the coast still going. The firemen are "mopping up."

In the papers, an interview with the Director of the Hans Christian Andersen Centre in Denmark: "I don't believe any really great literature is being written in Europe or North America today, literature is not really dangerous anymore. But Andersen is still dangerous."

A picnic in the park. Windy day, hot, the harbour a whitish, hazy postcard with all the modern buildings, surreal, gigantic totem poles of a mechanized civilization. Amazing how the shapes remain the same.

Michael in a good mood, discussing his stay in the Middle East. The Arabs, an impossibly passionate people, no, impossibly intense people, their eyes turn to eggplant purple when they become passionate.

A documentary on Celibadache, the Romanian conductor, on his first visit to Romania since he left in the late thirties.

Then a marvelous old film in black and white, showing him when young conducting the Berlin Philharmonic. An approach to music full of finesse, total involvement. How difficult it is to define what music is. Sounds can remain sounds or become music. Out of a hundred concerts three or four maybe in which the music comes alive in a real way, a phenomenon that cannot be predicted, but comes out of a group effort.

Régine Crespin singing Berlioz's *Nuits d'été* . . . especially absence—an ineffable sadness.

FEBRUARY

We traveled down to visit Jane. Very hot. We stopped at Gosford to have a drink. The streets empty, drained people like us traveling. The rocks were glistening on the Newcastle Express and the road seemed wet, a mirage of heat and distance and the countryside lost in a misty haze, the earth cracking in the silence of the heat.

At Jane's the house cool, the cries of cockatoos. The sea, further down, abandoned houses everywhere in the ochre, silver bush, with the gums far up, their trunks made of polished rock.

The lorikeets in the trees full of magnificent colors, brilliant greens and reds, yellows, as if someone had gone over them with a brush.

Sharp, hollow sounds in the dry air, like Aboriginal sticks, the real sound of the landscape.

Reading Byron's *Ravenna Journal* of 1821. I was looking at the book hoping that he would say something about Greece, seeing that he was almost going there. But no, he is enmeshed in Italian political affairs, a nice, light, slightly ironic but civilized tone about himself and life. I quite liked the way he talks to himself, he reads a lot, full of quotations from the books, he talks a great deal about freedom, shoots daily and rides, offers his help to all conspirators. Mavrokordatos apparently invited him to take part in the Greek Revolution.

He seems quite modest in his tone and wise. Quite different from the cliché image of him—bad, mad and so on . . . He is telling himself that he is less bored now that he is growing older.

John rang last night. He wanted me to come and talk to his students about language. I, as always, feeling trapped by the idea of facing an audience. But later, I thought of a few things that I could tell them. Language is like a vast, magnificent edifice built by the constant effort of successive generations of people, a day-by-day effort.

A language is a way of life, a perspective, it carries with it moral, factual, historical and aesthetic assumptions, a social approach, an attitude to people, relations, politics, life and death.

It is a thing alive, the moment one stops having a direct relation to it, a relation between the actual, immediate experience and the form that will translate it accurately, it becomes dead, cliché, dogmatic. A lot of present media usage, especially in advertising, shows nothing but this totally dead aspect which they try to enliven with images, color, noise.

Language circumscribes all our thinking processes, but all major works of art transcend the medium they use, bring to life new forms and new understandings.

Very hot. A glassy stillness over the city, the streets. Outside, the air as if coming out of an overheated oven. The nights depressingly hot and humid.

MARCH

The rain has stopped, the sun is shining and an amazing silence everywhere.

"Absence of willed noise," as Cage would say. I remember his visit a long time ago when James brought him to the Music Centre. A warm, ironic, philosophical tone, discussing his life, his attitude to music. How pleased he was that in dictionaries mushroom is followed by music, as he likes them both. Interested in people working together on an equal basis. How he discovered that he was not very good at harmony, but "noise" fascinated him. The soundproofed chamber at the university that he went in. He was told that there would be no sound in it at all, yet, he could hear two sounds, a very high one and one continuous low. The sound engineer told him that the high sound was his nervous system, and the low, the sound of his blood.

Last night at the drawing classes. An old building up this rickety staircase to the top, the walls peeling, tables full of paints.

The group around me silent. But the objects very deceptive and difficult to draw. Round oranges that seemed to have straight sides, paper cones that looked as if made of marble, black bottles that were full of white reflections, the interrelationship between them and the space impossible to catch. Here I was constantly measuring to discover how far away I was from their positions.

All mediums equally deceptive.

APRIL

A documentary on Pollock, his friends very good, elderly now. Analytical points by critics, biographers, curators, how he became a myth, the art scene in America needed an American hero. All the Abstract Expressionists at the time were foreign born: de Kooning, Rothko, Gorki. Pollock was the only one from Wyoming. They needed a name and they found it. Quoting one biographer: "It finally destroyed him, this terrible attention that he became dependent on, but which constantly demanded more and more production from him, was never satisfied . . ."

Sunday afternoon, the sun going down. The palm tree waiting in the last sunrays, a pale electric glow. Max on the roof near the chimney, waiting, his flanks like heavy silk on the dark iron roof and the radio playing: "Love is a many-splendored thing . . ."

The light full of a muted sadness, time, the element that we cannot keep still, that we cannot recapture, the image of this passing forever chilling.

TV language. This boring singer described as having: an awesome talent. On the sports fields men making heroic efforts with some ball. One becomes quite cynical about this inflated language, images of heroic men in shorts. Even Homer, in the Iliad, had to bring in the gods to make a fight appear more important. When in fact one had a large group of quarrelsome men playing out these games to the detriment of everyone and themselves.

Today we drove up toward the mountains. I suddenly remembered the last time I drove here with U. We were going up to visit the lawyer and his beautiful garden. We were driving fast on the empty, open road, suddenly this feeling that we will never be together again, the exact knowledge that struck as we were speeding, open fields on both sides of the road, the leaves of trees turning yellow, a golden air around us and the distance.

A feeling of suspension that lasted briefly, and the accurate knowledge that this was the last time it was going to happen. Looking at each other in a sudden togetherness. I both inside and outside the car, as if I were on the other side of the road, speeding in the opposite direction, disconnected from my own body, and watching us from outside, floating.

In the lawyer's garden we sat on the stone steps under the very old trees. The light filtered through the branches.
Thinking again about this constant question being asked: "What audience are you writing for?"

But if you look at the process of writing, the core of a piece sets its own directions, has its own necessities, imposes intrinsic values, interrelated actuality that must be found for the piece to come alive.

This has nothing to do with the audience except in the most generalized terms, you being that audience, hoping that there are others like you to become an audience.

To bend all these to the idea of an outside audience, market necessities, is as unreal as it is remote. And then in what terms can an audience be defined? This is not journalism that writes specifically for an editorial line and out of factual necessities.

MAY

Parsifal on SBS. Looking at these overhyped productions, embarrassingly twee somehow, overbloated heroes, sentiments, false heroics. Historic presentation of the theater, its construction in Beyreuth, the Hitler period. Unbearable really. I switched it off. One thinks of Rossini and his assessment of Wagner: "There are some fine movements in Wagner, but some terrible quarter hours."

Yet life seen from this point of view, masters with god-like powers and directions, women who must obey or are the mistress of the Devil, all this can only lead to the wrong basis for life. An inflated victory over nothing leading everyone to death and destruction.

It is as if no one wants to remember who they are, escape into some fantasy land. They don't want to know where they came from, what has been achieved so far. They all want to forget, be entertained, become like machines. A desire for death. While before, the memory of the tribe, the past, the knowledge that had been acquired so that they could survive, was considered of great importance, was passed on as a sacred duty.

People like oracular voices even when the message is hollow. Something reassuring about the tone, as if some distilled wisdom on which they can rely.

Crowded dreams of Latin American faces, the poverty, the abuse, the killings. A documentary by Frankovich. His documentaries have that interesting, unfinished look. The photography is always not too perfect, or the colors, you can never be distracted from the topic by aesthetic concerns.

The face of power not very nice, the church, the military, the upper-class politicians, all spouting biblical quotes, leaving them in the air, shields behind which they could indulge in anything they wanted to do. The Cardinal saying the church is a place of discipline and that if he had not joined the church, he would have joined the army. He liked discipline.

The President's voice sounded as if produced by a mechanical instrument inside his throat. A strangulated, whizzing voice, that arrived not as if directly articulated, but as a resonance of a surreal kind of voice inside him.

A satirical documentary on McDonald's. The singer outside a hamburger shop in Costa Rica, giving us this biting song about a calf told by its mother to be good, waiting for its rewards, and then the day came when he flew to the USA, four legs to California, his head to Detroit and his insides to the European Market. The ultimate in internationalism.

A representative of the firm, with a long, lugubrious face, was telling us how 40 million people were eating their products, of unlimited expansion possibilities, the ultimate commercial nirvana.

John Updike in the interview, he talked out of his established reputation. Reputations—something one must avoid at all costs.

They came for lunch yesterday, they brought photos of the family, our old friends. We had all grown old, with white hair, had lost our enthusiasm.

We talked of our dead, this incredible mystery, these new states we knew nothing of before, we could not imagine. And now, our own people struck down, and we helpless, unnerved by this watching, by our own impotence.

Reality—it establishes its own truth independently of an inner imagined one, that one carries for a long time and brings forward to impose on it. It is at the same time more terrible, more modest, more self-absorbed, more at ease, more indifferent than anything one imagines.

Greek folk song: "Death, let us fight on the marble threshing floor—let us struggle . . ."

Lost Edens, by Tennessee Williams. Technically very good, beautifully designed production, full of details, atmosphere, but the essence, a soap opera, awkward and unreal people, a sort of cliché of his earlier writing, the same type of wild, unexplained creatures, the women—oversexed, overpossessive, overblown.

The space between real emotion and sentimentality is so narrow that it is almost invisible.

Very hot and humid night, the house waiting in an oppressive silence. Dreamt of old women in black, white starched sheets, with slight holes, someone had died, and I was very sad. I kept putting the needle through the whiteness . . .

JUNE

Winter. Dark early and cold. A program on the ABC about the Ganges. The man introducing it described the river as: The essence of compassion in liquid form.

Reading a review by Peter Pierce of Motion's biography of Philip Larkin: ". . . the portrait emerges of a wilfully diminished life, which in its emotional thrift, personal meanness, resolute self-absorption, want of expansiveness, cherishing of the meagre and uneventful, seems emblematic of post-war Britain. This could well describe his poetry."

Fog and overcast. Too many deaths this year. I was telling Joan that I find these things difficult to take and that I insist that my friends stay well, and what is more important—ALIVE . . . She was laughing. Remembered Noel Coward when old, having lunch with a friend, remarking that the only thing he could ask a friend now, was to stay alive while having lunch with him.

We both laughed. We have not reached that point yet . . . I said . . . but it is coming . . . coming . . .

A letter in the weekend papers applauding an article about the well-known poet and ending: "We should celebrate this TITAN of the typewriter while we still have him in the flesh."

In the Strand Arcade the antique shop was full of the workmanship of the past. Delicate crystal beads, evening materials that seemed made by human hands, silver foxes, ethereal pinks, and the Strand Arcade at rest, like a noble animal that watches life go by, the light filtering through the glass roof and onto the cherry-red wood.

At the Opera House to see *Lady Macbeth of Mtsensk*. Shostakovich, written in 1934, he was young at the time, twenty-eight, I think. The proletariat on stage, the bourgeoisie, lots of sex, hate, vulgarity. The production not that involving in a dramatic sense, but the orchestral score inventive, young, full of energy, comic effects, pastiche.

One could see the new energies emerging in Russia after the Revolution. A rough-and-ready approach, but the music very interesting, full of effects, amazing that people at the time liked it so much, the audience here not ready for it seventy years later. We are constantly fed on nineteenth-century opera.

Dream. I was walking with someone at dusk. A bell began to toll. I said to the other person: "If we were in Greece, it would mean that someone had died."

Suddenly above us a group of black birds flew, large and very beautiful. They landed on a tree. A lot of movement. We stopped and watched them against the sky, silver black in the light, they were shaking their wings, which were pointed, like the spires of churches in Prague, silver black in the night.

JULY

Waiting for the gallery to open we went into the corner pub to have a drink. An old-fashioned place, rather run-down, with the eternal red carpet with large motifs, now half eaten away. Plastic chairs with a bad Bauhaus influence, and two large television sets, that could not be heard above the noise.

A politician's head appeared on one, his lips moving. Then the commercials came on in which young women's bottoms, in very low-cut bathing costumes were being exposed. They looked bronzed beyond belief, round beyond belief. The women displaying a sort of half-brutal, half-sporty approach to their bodies. An artificial, directed approach to conform to some idea of womanhood of advertisers.

Advertising—a sort of infantilism.

Driving from Canberra, coming down toward the lake, the sun setting, this marvelous presence in luminous blue grays. A light brushstroke over the horizon that changed as we moved, to a silvery blue, the hills above hardly any substantiality.

Thinking of Ola and death
how silent it comes
how discreet
how self-sufficient . . .
Death—foam over the sand in the twilight.

Looking at our lives, this brief performance, this involvement in an everyday that when it cuts, everything is out—views, evaluations, awareness.

Olive Cotton, her photographs so subtle, her whites ethereal, as if imagined whites. By comparison Dupain appears rougher, more energy perhaps, some hard core at the center of his photos, equally impressive, but with hers—a floating quality of light.

A documentary on Alfred Schnittke, the Russian composer. He was discussing his approach to music, he is trying to grasp things which are difficult to express, music being nearer to this possibility, a feeling, a suggestion, bringing it all together to catch the mystery of life, dying, life as it is, simple and enigmatic.

Discussing the idea of intellectually approaching the creative process. If one could catch the essence of things intellectually, one would express them intellectually. But in art, he felt, the essence is captured without defining it. "One is formed by one's life," he said, "yet in some way independent of one's time."

At the Greek sculpture exhibition. The sculptures in semi-darkness, with a strong, unreal light on them. They were waiting there in silence, in their tight, uneasy spaces. I wondered what they thought of all this.

On the wall, this marvelous votive plaque of a young man half-smiling, so fresh, so naive, so young. One is moved to see how a well-caught line can travel and survive for 2,500 years.

AUGUST

In Darwin for the Word and Breath Festival. I arrived at midnight. The hotel near the Parliament House, a square massive temple lighted in the night.

Darwin a city at ease, growing in every direction, full of trees, but not regimented. Heavy tropical plants. One is struck by the half nakedness of the people in the street.

In the mall, Aboriginal people gathered around the old tree, laughing, talking, socializing. Marvelous black skins, the women thin, wearing brilliantly colored blouses with large yellow or blue flowers, as if coming out of a Ray Crooke painting.

The hotel not too cleaned or restored, a feeling of real life about it. In the foyer, under glass, the photo of Mrs. Paspalis, and above it a painting of the bombing of Darwin, soldiers' metal hats with nets covering them, jungle gear.

Hot and humid, the fans humming, the palm trees swaying, young men and women swimming in the pool, coming out with dripping hair, ordering large portions of prawns, chips and beer.

In the evenings, a singer and an electric-guitar player, imitations of the husky, passionate tones of jazz singers.

Birut took me to Hawkins Place outside the city. Wallabies looking at us with interest, but running away the moment we came out of the car. Walking through the bush, heavy tropical plants, gigantic roots made of solid rope hanging from the branches, tree trunks built in waves of colors, batik paintings in red and brown.

And then the BRUSH TURKEY, the most marvelous creature, black, with an oval head, set on its somehow triangular body, as if a piece of sculpture by Miro, walking with an almost human walk, slightly awkward.

Birut said that they live in nests built over a number of generations, one on top of the other. A vision of dark elegance in the bush.

At night we went for dinner at the wharf, with Birut, Dirk and Sylvia, a lively woman from Alice, telling us how afraid she had been of the sea when she saw it for the first time, when she came to Darwin as a young woman.

We ate fish, of course, the sun setting in spectacular colors, then the night, the waters dark, the lights of the city far away, and the oil rig, a magic tree, lighted, floating in the sea.

We walked to the reading in the Town Hall Ruins with Barry Hill. He looking very elegant in his light suit, talking of his last trip to the Centre, the book he was working on.

The night warm, a half-moon, dogs barking from time to time and Brown's Mart full of lights.

The Aboriginal writers, reading, singing their poems, accompanied by guitars, stories of displacement—Bobby Randall, Herbie Langton.

Herb Wharton, an ironic, laconic view of life. He was sporting a cane. An interesting-looking face, bushy eyebrows, a hat, a dusted color to his clothes and his eyes only partly opening as of people who had lived long in hot places where the sun is strong. But when he took his hat off, his eyes were very soft, sad and human, a charged pair of eyes, as of someone who had done a lot of inner living.

Traveling with them the next day to the Dudley Point reading, in the bus, a lot of jokes about crocodiles, maybe they should put together a book of Aboriginal crocodile jokes . . .

Then the TREES, they all noticed them, some of them with sacred meanings. They were mapping them as if they were real beings. Herbie Langton, the storyteller, referring to the plum tree as "my tree."

SEPTEMBER

Looking at the Literary Grants applications, some five hundred of them, I became despondent, the whole country seemed to be applying for grants, but slowly, reading them, one became amused, enthusiastic, moved by the direction, the urgency, the pleading quality of applications. A nakedness about them. Some writers had developed amazing intellectual vocabularies to describe what they intended to do, using the latest critical theories, new stylistic approaches.

The process of applying already unbalancing one's tone, trying to imagine what approach to take, who are these people looking at applications.

A poet describing the direction of his writing: "My poetry has been moving toward a transformation of the lyric and the genre toward more paratactic forms. See for example my poem 'The Goanna Inheritance.'"

In the bus going to town. Two young people in the seat in front of me. He with dark curly hair and glasses. She with light brown hair falling over the seat in front of me. They were talking in quiet voices, looking at lecture notes.

He was reading her face, moving his head from side to side as if a text to which he was giving all his attention, interest, listening to the reverberations of her voice. Nodding approvingly. Taking everything in with great care, bending over her shoulder delicately to look at some lines.

Inscribed on a bus seat—*I love Irfan.*

A bulbul in the garden is attacking the water in the dish with little jumps, listening to some conversation in the trees.

When we came back from shopping I prepared Mavis's favourite dish—potatoes in the oven with lemon, olive oil and paprika. She greeted them enthusiastically as they came out of the oven.

I said: "Maybe I should write an ode to potatoes."

We laughed. It was cozy in the kitchen, the rain and the wind outside were blowing fiercely, the garden full of pine needles, and in the morning a chorus of kookaburras. A most unusual sound in this neighborhood.

Stormy night. Brisk walk to the Opera House. Sydney wet and beautiful in the night, full of golden lights, the sea. Inside a performance of Verdi's *Macbeth.*

The sets large and heavy, cumbersome, props that had gathered dust and had been resurrected for the occasion. The costumes elaborate, rich but also heavy. The men wearing armour and battle headgear and everywhere banners being carried.

Something shallow and bravado about the whole performance, and the singers could not match the scale of the production except by bravado performances. Poor Verdi.

Lady Macbeth, full of prance but little subtlety, her voice good, her top notes sent shivers down your spine, yet the voice with an uneasy surface, lacking in dramatic control and tension. Nothing came from inside, a throat voice with little to back it.

The whole performance totally unmoving, one could not care less about their fate, and however much they washed their hands, no inner blood had been spilled there.

A blockbuster sort of an evening, we clapped and laughed a great deal and went away as after a circus performance, amazed at the tricks, but as regards the human drama, as far away from the stage as possible.

Driving out for the day, past Kiama we saw this abandoned open mine of basalt, the most amazing Dantesque sight. A small inlet with waters pounding sheer walls of black rock, looking like columns from the underworld. The surface of the sea exploding with light.

The quarry closed now, the wind very strong, further out walls and walls of cut basalt, rock formations about the sea.

OCTOBER

So hot since yesterday. Last night a summer night, with a moon and the scent of honeysuckle in the air. The night, curtains of dark feathers. The strong shadow of the chimney on the terrace floor.

Dream. A burning ceremony, some ritual, a test I had to pass, unclear in the dream. A fire burning on the ground. I had to throw this green cloth on the fire. The cloth seemed alive, talking, making some kind of complaint, lament. I was very agitated, could not understand why I had to do it. A short man was picking up the pieces of the cloth from the ashes, putting them on his chest and singing.

The pieces had acquired beautiful colors, burnished greens, blues, as if velvet.

Birds in the garden everywhere, big and small. The magpies have taken to coming regularly, they walk with dignity on their thin legs, drink water from the dish, dip their heads, take a mouthful of water and then raise their heads to the sky, and back again.

Earlier, a large sulfur-crested cockatoo was walking on the garden path. A solid body that moved awkwardly on the ground, placing one foot in front of the other as if wearing rubber flippers.

Looking at old papers, letters. The past—I find it very tiring now, before it seemed a consolation.

On the political scene, the media, visits from presidents, politicians, nothing is being quoted or discussed but economic advantages, no other angle of information. They are sure that GREED will get us all interested, observant, pliant.

Mark returning from overseas, discussing the old country: "They changed their friends, but not their beliefs, however wrong history had proved them. To change their beliefs would have been tantamount to death."

Rereading Seferis's journals. Describing his childhood, traveling to Skala in summer—"the sun is setting over the Two Brothers; twilight spreads across the sky, the color of an inexhaustible love . . ."

Later, in Paris, with Maro, having a bouillabaisse soup, he asks the waiter what fish they had used, and the waiter replies: "Ce sont des poissons propices à la bouillabaisse." And Seferis: ". . . I liked the word 'propice' at that hour of sacred rite."

Goethe's translation of a moral fable quoted by the Persian poet Nizami—1141–1203:

> Jesus and his disciples were passing by a marketplace and suddenly, at some distance from the street, they saw the carcass of a dog with a crowd of curious people around it. One said, "This stench drives me insane." And another: "Refusal to bury this will only bring misfortune." Jesus also observed the carcass and said:
>
> "The teeth are beautiful, like white pearls."
>
> His glance remained on the only thing which was beautiful amid the rot, on the teeth's whiteness. And all blushed with shame, for they had learned to see only what was evil and ugly.

NOVEMBER

Beautiful hot day. Scent of trees in bloom. The shadow of the pine tree on the garden path. Bird discussions in the trees. The street empty.

Small, young sparrows are jumping in flanks across the lawn, as if some dance. They come to the water dish, jump nervously on the rim, look fast in all directions before dipping into the water.

Dream last night, the fear so palpable that it woke me. It seemed I was present at a murder. Enclosed, totally white room, views in through a door, a trapdoor. A man and a woman, heads unseen, the man's body into view as if a paper cut-out.

In the middle of his chest a series of square openings, semi-transparent windows. They slid across, moved, closed, the milky transparent color of a television screen. The feeling that if they opened totally, you would be able to see the view at the back of the man.

A tension in the room. Then the woman approached. She had a gun in her hand, she pressed it against his body. At the gesture, I woke up, sure that it will fire.

The night very silent.

More and more published books each year, more and more prizes, more and more geniuses, one every week almost. I, at least, can't keep up with them. One assumes that the entire system, publishers, critics and so on, to use Nadar's euphemism, are part of a harmonized system.

Reading Nicholas Shakespeare's biography of Chatwin, he is quoting Rizzoli, his Italian publisher, describing

Chatwin, "His morality was totally aesthetic, built on the best inks, but not with blood."

At the Nimrod. The walls full of posters of past performances, one of Jim McNeil's play *How Does Your Garden Grow?* The last time I met him was at a preview of his play. He looked thin, suntanned with warm brown eyes of a friendly nocturnal animal. Telling me that he drank to escape it all and made a nuisance of himself. Never again. He was smoking his Gitanes, speaking with a wheezing voice.

We sat up high on the last row in the theater. He became tense every time a policeman appeared on stage, in his own play, swearing at them.

The play, the characters, immediate and human. Very complex and subtle use of language. A homemade product with smell, taste and lyricism. A unique talent on the Australian scene, I feel, he and Kenna.

Real insights into the Australian soul. An everyday soul full of domestic details. Clean humour, vulnerable, lacking in coarseness. A magnificent utilisation of current clichés and all that *Readers Digest* philosophy.

What he made plausible at all times was that people in prison are like us and we are like them, how a society and its time penetrates everything, in the same manner, how we all live by the same things, independently of where we are.

And of adjustments to situations, makeshift as they may be. The things that we are bringing into our lives to make the everyday domestic, to relieve boredom, to give ourselves a *sense of security, and of power over our lives.*

The irony of all this was that a man who had come in contact with so much violence and had seen human beings from such angles, should produce human characters, while the generation outside were writing clinical, technical plays.

DECEMBER

We were at the exhibition, the celebrity opening the show spoke fulsomely of the young painter, his career, his travels, describing him as "traveling excessively."

The young painter seemed at ease with this fulsomeness. He was dressed de rigueur, in his jeans and black leather jacket. But his paintings on the walls were pure tourist brochure stuff.

We left in a hurry and went for dinner at No Names. A real place with wooden tables, good Italian bread, at-ease waiters.

At the tables, a different race of people, shaped by darker forces, were eating their pastas, drinking the golden cordial. We joined in, pleased to be out of the gallery.

Dinner on the island. The candles burnt out during the meal. Our faces more like presences at the table. Something familiar yet disconnected about the atmosphere.

When we left, we came down by torch and moonlight through the shredded trees, far down, the sea like a lake, and that silence that pursued us, enveloped us from everywhere.

Then we all got into the small, aluminum boat, paper cut, on the dark, powerful, massive waters. The boat bending every time another person got in, precariously moving away from the pier, so that when we were all in it, it sunk to the level of the waters, a black mirror full of dark blue glints, stretching far along the coastline. I thought for a moment what would happen if we all sunk.

Then the motor started and for a few seconds we advanced rapidly, then the motor would die down, and Rudi would take the only oar in the boat and row for a few seconds, like a gondolier, then he would start the motor again, the boat shooting momentarily over the surface, then sinking back as the motor died. I was too fascinated by the whole thing to remember my fear, watching the golden lights on the other side that we hoped to reach.

Finally we made it. We walked down the abandoned road, to our cars, past the she-oaks, the smell of the sea everywhere, talking of fear, the sea.

And I remembered going with Father, when I was small, in summer, to the beach on the other side of the city, crossing the Danube by boat with a boatman rowing. The empty stretch of sand, golden white in the strong summer sun, and at the back of it a forest of willow trees, the river alive with sparkling explosions of light.

Then Father dived in and was gone. I watched for what seemed an interminable time for him to surface, but he was not coming up. I became more and more alarmed, frightened, then a total panic took hold of me as I watched this golden surface of the river, the strong light on it flowing too.

I had started to cry when Father emerged, surprised . . .

JOURNAL VIII

JANUARY

New Year. The fireworks began and the ships, baritones and basses, vocalizing in the night from the very bottom of their throats, their dark stomachs. The evening marvelous, warm and crisp with a slight wind. One could hear people's voices from the other side of the park.

Reading Delacroix's journal. A lot of discussions about *beauty*, what is beauty, the beautiful—"idealized truth":

> Paris 1st January, 1861
>
> I began the new year by going on with my work at Saint Sulpice, as usual I have paid no visits, except by leaving cards, which is no trouble to me, and I have been working all day long. What a good life! What a divine compensation for my solitary state, as they call it! Brothers and fathers, relatives and friends of all kinds

> live together, quarrelling and hating, and scarcely able to say a sincere word to one another. Painting, it is true, like the most exacting of mistresses, harasses and torments me in a hundred ways.
>
> For the last four months I have been getting up at dawn, and hurrying off to this enchanting work as though I was rushing to throw myself at the feet of a beloved mistress. What seemed so easy at a distance, has now become dreadfully and unceasingly difficult. But how is it that this unending struggle revives instead of destroying me and, far from discouraging, comforts me and occupies my mind when I leave it?
>
> A blessed compensation for all that has gone with my youth! A noble occupation for the old age that is already assailing me in so many ways, but still leaves me enough strength to overcome bodily suffering and the ills of the spirit.

Delacroix died two years later.

Last night we saw a documentary on the Armenian genocide, no one talks about it, they are being told that they are imagining it, this is why the Jewish people are laboring at it, for fear that in a little while everyone will say that it is a figment of their imagination. The twentieth century has seen how everything can be wiped out, from books, records, memory.

Nadezhda Mandelstam going over the same fact to establish it beyond doubt, through several sources, angles, this amazing detailed attention to the smallest fact. It moved me when I read *Hope Against Hope*. People fighting to keep the memory of things alive, because they imply lives that have irrevocably been lost, that have no other means to survive but that of memory.

A crisp morning, the streets deserted, as if the city is uninhabited, not even dogs. A lonely pigeon walking down the garden path. The same one who visits often, I assume, and who was having a bath in the rain one morning on the electricity line, wiping each feather clean with its beak, like a person washing a blade carefully, and then putting delicately, one of its claws in one ear and shaking its head, in the funniest way. The whole procedure with enormous care.

Max Kozloff, American critic:

> There is a fundamental difference between a photograph and a painting from an evidential point of view. A photograph is a trace of something that once existed, a residue of light. In effect, it is a refuge from a moment that was.
>
> . . . a painting, to the contrary, is a sovereign over a moment that never was, in fact, created. A painting is always a hypothesis, no matter how assiduously it relates to something we know or remember.

FEBRUARY

In Hyde Park, passing the Archibald Fountain, walking to the Gallery, I remembered the morning I went with Mother to see the exhibition. The gallery cool and empty. Lee Hobbs's monumental *Miss Luna* smiled good-naturedly out of her protruding teeth, her hat with flowers, her enormous bosom, the painted, fresh crust of her personality.

She was all colors, a candy-made *Miss Luna.*

As we came back through the park, Michael was standing, tall and lonely on the other side of the fountain. He bowed very politely to shake Mother's hand and then watched her with a discreet curiosity, as if of another world that held some interest for him. But he was inwardly preoccupied, someone had abandoned him there, and he was contemplating an empty future.

Sunday night, very hot and humid, stifling. I could not sleep. I thought of the photographer—Penny Tweedie. She arrived promptly at three. She had come down from the Top End where she was doing an assignment. Pale, suntanned face, no concession to coquetry, her blonde hair parched by the heat, the wind.

All her gestures at one with the profession she was exercising—one felt that she could load cameras in her sleep, moved very fast once she caught the frame, the angle, the gesture, the position, the air. A pleasure to watch.

We went to the Rocks where she took photos in an ancient doorway, people passed, stopped to watch the object of this attention, the process still a mystery, so that they went suddenly quiet around us, not to interrupt it.

When the photos arrived we looked and looked at them, like an addiction, to see one's image, to be reassured. Later, when I looked in the mirror, it was my face in the photographs that looked back at me. The camera and its ability to steal one's personality.

Penny was saying that the strength of the Aboriginal people seems to be in their secrecy, but that we must all go and see the Centre.

A program on television about Africa. The Africa inside us. The bush, the animals walking gracefully and full of dignity, well balanced and holding themselves at the exact center of things. The deer, turning their elaborate heads as if beautiful young women in a drawing room. The lion, who apparently, or so the speaker was telling us, is modest in his demands, generous in his approach, kills only when hungry, a family man, yet an individual.

A perfect personality as far as I could make out.

Helen Vendler discussing *The Strength of Poetry*, the Oxford lectures given by James Fenton:

> A writer's struggle with language, genre and poetic structure is his or her exasperating, obsessive and often heroic way of getting the themes to stay put. Otherwise, expressed in ordinary and undistinctive language they just melt away.
>
> This struggle with means is at least as important to the writer's life as any moral struggle. Fenton is willing to look at the moral struggle (politics, sex) but not at the linguistic one. Whereas the aesthetic drive locks the two together, Fenton separates them. An aesthetic object is intriguing precisely because the two struggles, moral and linguistic, must become in it a single pursuit. Delete one struggle and the interest fades.

MARCH

Long night, very hot, dogs barking, furtive, secret cars passed down the street stopped somewhere close, yet unseen, the moon out in a humid sky. Restless, thinking of a hundred things, all the impressions from the trip to Newcastle, flying in this small plane, quite empty. They gave us very good coffee, the aroma drifting while we watched the landscape below, flying somehow very close to the ground. The NSW coastline dotted with semi-precious stones, sliced, the fine veins could be seen, in round or elongated shapes in vivid turquoise blue, or mud greens, mustard yellows. And the sea like wrinkled fine sheets of paper, the boats near the shore small, white specks reflected on green grass transparency.

And then the evening with the Smiths. He was small, dark and nervous, with a twisted sort of energy, she was keeping a close watch on him to see that everything was not too much, like an over-anxious mother, they were minding the house for a year. Other people's taste, lifestyle, marking the place.

He was saying that when he first came to Australia, he was sent on an archeological survey. Fire places, he was saying are eternal things, people come back to the same spots, smelling the human, as other animals would smell their own. And this night, both he and the girl botanist involved in the survey, were asleep in their sleeping-bags, when suddenly, the girl in her nightdress, rushed to him, held him by the hand, a terror that passed through her, transmitted itself to him, or came to him at the same time, this force that was menacing, he felt wanted to destroy them and at that moment the only thing he could do was cry out, some primeval cry that distorted their faces, covered their terrible trembling. It took them a long time to recover.

Cool autumn weather. The birds exercising for their major trip. The air crisp and above the line of the horizon a hazy mist, the houses rising out of it.

At the launch of the book, the poet, short and square, with a suntanned face and worried look about him, kept on passing his hand through his hair. After the speeches, while sipping wine, he was telling me that the bottom had fallen out of the poetry market and that he was now writing novels. He had just finished one, was unsure of it.

Afternoon tea, the kitchen full of light, the sky beautifully blue, Max stretched out close to the wall to catch the breeze under the gate, the radio on, and Mrs. Crawford has totally disappeared, a box of ashes now waiting under her dining room table to be taken to England.

Her presence in the house next door such a continuous and persistent fact and now, no one on the balcony to complain about the neighborhood.

From time to time her daughter puts out in the street some unwanted object, yesterday an old pair of shoes with a prim aspect to them.

Slowly all the objects she was clinging to will go, disappear, become part, maybe of someone else's everyday, the house with new owners.

APRIL

Vanessa Redgrave discussing playing, acting, roles, etc. . . . "You have to find the voltage that will bring the character to life and then maintain it, this is why it is so exhausting."

Last night we went to see the *Noah Plays*, two short ones. Both spectacular. Marvelous costumes, dance-like movements, a mixture of silence, static poses with sudden outbursts of energy. Enormously controlled and taxing performances. The music—stringed instruments, drums and sticks, the voice of the narrator chant-like, giving the actors their singing tones.

A subtle combination of colors, sounds, movements executed with great virtuosity. The fabrics of the costumes superb rich textures that added to the monumentality of the movements.

But I found it uninvolving in spite of all the tragedies portrayed. The *Living Monument* gave a long, well-sustained performance. But when he laughed, his mouth was all black, a dark cavity that made one shiver, as if seeing a ghost.

In an article in *The New York Review of Books* about an exhibition of Max Beckmann's work. They were quoting him: "The essential meaning of space or volume is identical with individuality, or that which humanity calls God. For in the beginning there was space, that frightening and unthinkable invention of the Force of the Universe."

Watching *A Piano Century*—a program on European pianists, these short, compact men, with small, energetic hands, an attitude in their bodies, their heads that somehow reminded me of Father.

MAY

After weeks of discussions, Jurgis has devised our new short trip and we are on our way to Lightning Ridge.

Approaching Coolah, the fields golden brown fur, falling over under the delicate blue sky. At Coolah Heights, undulating hills, dark rich brown full of trees, their shadows chasing each other down the hill as in the painting by Edwin Pareroultja from Hermannsburg.

At night, dinner in the Coolah Café, full of the noise of the television permanently on. Ugly ceramic objects on display for sale, plants, paintings. The food to match. We talked of the past. Europe. The war. Cousins, uncles sent to Siberia, released after many years, coming back as broken people.

Toward Walgett. Clouds floating in the gauze of the sky as if held in liquid. The mulgas appearing, delicate and looking as if out of medieval tapestries. The horizon totally open on both sides of the road, space, the soil ochre red, the sky a giant dome, constantly changing.

Lightning Ridge—the feeling of an improvised town, small buildings, miners everywhere in dungarees, opals, and a lot of energy. The sky at dusk, dark, blue black, like the black opal. No stars.

Dinner at the Lightning Ridge Motel. At the bar a young man looking like a nineteenth-century Calvinistic icon, thin face, long, pointed black beard, drinking with another, short with round arms and heavy legs, both dusted with underground dirt.

We visited the *Bush Mooseum*, an amazing amalgam of all the paraphernalia of living in Lightning Ridge—rusted objects, machinery, skeletons of cars, faded newspaper articles, bottles and bottles, all arranged and looking as if a dust-encrusted still life by Morandi.

Then in the underground more surprising objects, a French legionnaire's bayonet, samovars, balalaikas, Elvis Presley records and Slim Dusty singing *The Pub with No Beer.* Everything dusty and yellowed with time, the times and heroics of the whites, the only mention of the Aboriginal people was a man who had killed a white woman.

A lot of practical ingenuity about their lives. The houses built out of any available material, the balalaika, the resonance box made out of a night pot, yet the sound seemed okay.

It began to rain during the night, a soft, gentle rain. The trees very pleased, moving, shaking their manes. In the washroom, the women pleased too. No rain since January.

The names of the streets: Onyx Street, Brilliant, Gem, Opal, Agate, Silica Street.

Late one afternoon we discovered the Mary and Paul Bird studio. The walls full of strong, colorful painting. Mary Bird speaking of arriving in Lightning Ridge thirty years earlier, as a young woman, just married. When the first child was born, she would go down to the diggings with her husband, the baby and papers, and spend the whole day down there to escape the intense heat, 42–45 above ground. They all emerged out at night.

Trying to find Black Opal House, closed it seemed, through the now muddy streets, we met this man driving a truck down a narrow dirt road. We asked for directions. And he: "You'd better turn to the main road, you don't want to be bushed here."

The only time I've come across the expression was in a poem by Randolph Stow, "The Land's Meaning":

But one who has returned, his eyes blurred maps
of landscapes still unmapped, gives this account:

"The third day, cockatoos dropped dead in the air.
Then the crows turned back, the camels knelt down
    and stayed there,
and a skin-colored surf of sandhills jumped the
    horizon
and swamped me. I was bushed for forty years . . ."

JUNE

Last night looking out of the window at the bridge, the lights, the cars moving along the curve of the bridge. I thought suddenly of this shrinking of the future that strikes one so suddenly while watching the cars going home in the early winter evening. Small, square lights suspended above the darkness. We are dying without knowing it, traveling toward a diminishing future.

Busy the whole weekend with the cupboard, cleaning after the painting, rearranging. Objects, OBJECTS, objects, more and more of them, suddenly totally overwhelmed by them, somehow they are becoming an imposition, a menace, a burden . . .

The bulbuls drinking water from the dish in the garden, raising their elaborate headgears in unison, as if medieval hats.

Watching a sentimental Greek film on television, the emotional dilemmas of the heroes put across through rembetika music.

But LOVE—remains always a mystery that constantly surprises us, tortures us, a miraculous happening that strikes suddenly out of the darkness. We are watching this sudden flowering surprised in spite of our cynicism.

Reading last night in a biography of Leopardi:

> Of Leopardi it might be said, as Baudelaire said of Pascal, that he carried his gulf with him, wherever he went. Both possessed that terrifying experience of the empty interstellar spaces, which find expression early in Leopardi's *L'Infinito* . . .
>
> For a religious mind like Pascal's this experience may be a preliminary stage toward a mystical purgation: for a mind rendered incapable by temperament or upbringing of entering into such a state, this experience can only erect a backdrop of total despair against which the human drama is enacted. Moreover, Leopardi's universe, is perhaps vaster and in a sense more terrifying than Pascal's.

Cold morning, smell of mist, traveling in the bus, images of England, the green fields as I was traveling to Manning Tree to see Miki, that biting air. People coming into the bus changed by the approaching winter, by the cold, the winter clothes taken out of mothballs, ill-fitting somehow, unironed, all of them looking like lost souls taking an unknown journey.

Elgar: "Music is all around us, and we can take as much as we like."

Jolanta's ceramic koala has arrived in the house. Part of a series of native animals she has been making. All very alive, a good balanced volume to their bodies and looking at ease.

Max comes through the house and suddenly notices the koala next to the fireplace. He approaches gingerly, smells it, goes around it, checks it, lies in the hall and watches it to see if it comes alive.

He is more often in the house now, demands more attention, runs through the corridor making unusual noises, then comes back to look at the sculpture, sniffs it, listens for any sort of movement through the ceramic skin, unconvinced by this stillness, a ploy maybe.

He looks away pretending to be indifferent, sprawls on the floor in front of it.

We are all pleased by this attention, we take Max's assessment as proof of our conviction of the vitality of the piece.

JULY

In the Mikhalkov film from a story by Chekhov. In the countryside, the train crossing in the early morning, the sun coming up, the white smoke in the distance and Chekhov watching it: "My God, how easy it is to be happy, sitting in a compartment, safe, having tea, speaking to a casual acquaintance . . ."

The pianist tonight, thin, aged, with glasses, his back curved, bending over the keyboard as if to collect some precious, indescribably precious stones, afraid to touch them lest they disappeared, transform under his touch, an arabesque of mesmerizing gestures over the piano. Preparing tense for the orchestra to finish the introduction, watching the conductor, short-sightedly, nervously.

But when the music erupted it was strong and masculine, evolving slowly into whirlpools of magic, wider and wider, till you forgot him, till the light that rose out of the music was filling the air, till everything disappeared and you were floating on music.

At John's for lunch. We stayed on the rocks above the water drinking champagne and orange juice. The sun on the water, like broken glass glinting, jumping the surface.

The tugs went by upright and dark like people sure of their purpose and slightly pompous about it. The garden full of sorrel, a family of small fish going around in circles below the film of green water. The air full of resonance. Everyone in a good mood.

I was watching the horizon behind their heads as the evening fell, somehow too rapidly, the delicate colors of the sky, and the houses turning to dark shadows, then the moon came up, like a Gustave Doré painting, in a sparkling midnight blue sky.

Raining constantly and cold. The crows calling out from the trees like people suffering, a harsh, lamenting sound in the pine trees.

The editor found my piece too small. Length, length is what they want. "You must write more," he said. "I can't," I said. He, incredulous: "What do you mean you can't?"

Everyone forgets that writing rises out of an inner necessity, that each piece has its own measure, determined by itself, which no one can alter without altering its nature.

A little criticism around and the air gets chilly immediately. One loses one's enthusiasm and the ability to write, the place becomes empty and one alone as usual, in front of this uninformed hostility.

Late, very late last night, watched a Russian film directed by Vladimir Bortko, of Bulgakov's *Heart of a Dog*.

I laughed a lot. Dear Bulgakov. I felt very pleased with him, as if he were my brother, at his magnificent achievement, how well everything worked, a Gogol of our times.

Very good, terrible, ferocious humour, an indictment of the communist system and of science, to a certain extent. A parable of scientific possibilities that overstep human boundaries, making a human out of a dog and then watching the terrible creature they have created.

Mordant ironies about the new class, house committees, communal singing, the old class, the arts scene . . .

AUGUST

Jim sent some poems and very lovely photographs of the Adelaide Hills, dark blond, red colors, the type of landscape that I love. Something modest and self-contained about these empty spaces that I have always found moving. They also remind me of Mother's essential nature—somehow.

Elizabeth over the phone, she had accepted to be writer-in-residence for three weeks. At an afternoon tea with members of the department, a staff member was telling her that: "the best thing about artists-in-residence is that very quickly it demystifies the artists."

Elizabeth in a marvelously stubborn voice: "It will take more than three weeks to demystify me."

Henry Moore's retrospective exhibition at the Art Gallery. Very beautiful, noble, human forms, monumental and yet intimate, full of amazing combinations of abstractions and representational forms. The drawings, the etchings, the use of gouache—white, red and green colors, amazingly delicate. The razor-edged bronze figure, in movement, the same feeling as of ancient Greek statues. A wind moving through the folds of the chiton.

The whole exhibition an inspiration and encouragement to see his achievement after sixty years and how he worked continuously, ideas that took ten years to come to fruition, ten years one realized suddenly, mean nothing in terms of inner development. The overwhelming feeling of continuous work—diaries, maquettes.

Inner discoveries and then the capability of finding a stylistic expression for it, the most tenuous of things, and yet so fundamental, a way of seeing life, feeling part of it. Magda Olivero's voice on the radio—immense palaces opening up in front of you, vistas of Renaissance elegance.

The moon for a few nights, very strong, the terrace as if bathed in blue sunlight, and she in the middle of the sky, high up, looking down with the face of a chubby doll, a smile on her face.

At the Opera House to hear the concert. Through the glass the harbour, a living thing, breathing in the dark, the lights made of clean cut glass.

Beethoven's Ninth Symphony. Listening to the sounds I remembered suddenly the concert in that year of disasters. By some terrible coincidence Richard and his new lover were sitting in the seats slightly in front of me. My utter desperation then, the music coming in waves, like a great flood in which I hoped I could drown, forget myself, acquire some immunity to life, reduce their importance, bring them to their normal size.

I met Mrs. Roberts at the bus stop. She was going to Palm Beach for the day. The fire of his death, her only son, still goes through her, she comes out for air, not to be consumed in the house by her grief.

It takes two hours from Wynyard. By the time she arrives it will be lunchtime. She will go into this place that serves Devonshire tea, hot scones, jam and cream, apple pies, eat something then take the bus back. It would be afternoon by the time she makes it back. Another day gone.

"Only forty-five," she said, "and his grandmother still alive at ninety-two."

She was going to Greece. A relationship there, her voice rising with the physical excitement. I thought afterwards that the body has its own language, independent of us.

SEPTEMBER

Spring day after the rain. The garden pleased, the air full of echoes of voices. The house resting. Life a series of domestic days with cats sitting in the shade and rose bushes full of buds.

"Poetry in translation," she said, "like a bird full of light on which they have suddenly attached lead weights. It keeps opening its wings, taking deep breaths and remains on the ground, unable to rise."

Reading Chamfort from time to time to balance one's view of current events: "Considering the general level of literature during these last ten years, literary celebrity, it seems to me, is by now a kind of disgrace which is not quite so damaging as the pillory, but soon will be."

"If it were not for the Government, one could not laugh at all now, in France."

"Posterity is nothing but one public which follows another. Well, you can see what the public is at the moment."

And all this at the end of the eighteenth century.

He was very angry with life, with people. Where was everyone? No one here to help him. I said: "We are getting older, have less energy. Time is passing." And he: "Time? Time? Where is Time? I can't see it."

I wanted to tell him Rilke's story about Time passing, imperceptibly, like a light wind over our faces . . .

In Brisbane for Writers' Week, at the Mayfair Hotel. The square in front of the Brisbane Town Hall packed with people waiting for the Broncos to arrive from Sydney, where they had won the match. Rock singers, noise, electrified bands, the warm night full of lights, the Town Hall in gold and red colors.

Shouts from the podium, the crowd shouts in response. The whole building is shaking, the bathroom, the fridge, the lifts are murmuring everywhere.

Chris drove us to the hotel after the session. Miroslav Holub in the car. Stories about the Russians, sinister anecdotes about Lenin's brain after he died, talk of the Eastern bloc, Romania . . .

Chris to me: "Of you it can be said that Romania has become ROO MANIA."

We all laughed.

Yesterday I watched a documentary on Akhmatova. Anatoly Naiman interviewed, a very interesting writer, describing Akhmatova during the long communist period. Language had become totally unreal, clogged with terrible things, like a sewer, he said, flowing over all things, and in the middle of this terrible current—Akhmatova—a small stone, covered, battered by all this, but maintaining its nature, holding on to the essentials.

What has always moved me is that when she was asked to speak over the radio to the women of Leningrad during the German siege of the city, she spoke of the Russian language, how they must save it, pass it on to the children. As if language was the essential core of the country and the struggle.

OCTOBER

At the evening of the presentation he was sitting at our table, an important personage, it seemed, involved in film. Very preoccupied inwardly and sour-looking.

He asked us all for our life measurements, who we were, what we had done and so on. On the defensive constantly, how much the Government was doing. I said I knew about it, I had worked in the arts too. Suddenly he began to shout that the industry did not owe anyone a living, and that if someone had not made it by the age of forty, he could only blame himself.

A mean-spirited, tight sort of individual, with a feeling of being constantly attacked, he was conducting business at the table, asking me, indifferently, if there are any ethnic people who could write for films. I made some remark about cultural difficulties, but he went on to discuss our inability to express our position . . .

I was silent. Who would want to discuss again these issues with all these cultural illiterates?

Watching television one forgets the marvelous wide world of the imagination, the intellect, the senses, the sensitivities of so many people that have enriched us. There is nothing there but the most promiscuous use of movement, violence, superficiality. We become like them, empty-headed, propaganda-prone, advertisement-riddled, sale-oriented.

A few weeks had passed since he had died. "On Monday," she said, "we will go back to the everyday."

She did not know that after such events, the everyday is an altered thing, that it hardly comes back, even later, in the same form, a total reconstruction, remaking of an everyday, on other premises and in other forms, this disappearance leaves total marks on everything.

Listening to *Pelleas and Melisande*, a strange, disturbing music, insinuating, seemingly soft, but with an amazingly disturbing and slightly sinister edge. One longed to get away from it, and yet come back. A very tragic tale played out in mysterious and dark environments. As if from the beginning, the heroes were dealing with obscure, dangerous forces, outside their capacity to control, but which came as in life, unnoticed, sweetly, as the French dancer used to say: "Doucement comme la mort."

At the Russian Club for the cultural event. The portrait of Lomonosov on the small stage, surrounded by flags and camellias from the neighboring gardens. At the long table covered with a brilliant red cloth, the three members of the cultural committee moved slightly in the rhythm of Mr. Pancharov's speech, the microphones as usual, not working. The machines always against us. Mrs. Andreyev was in green, with green earrings. She gave the impression of generosity.

Behind me older versions of Pasternak, the same blue-green eyes, trimmed hair and sharp cheekbones. I kept on looking behind me at the strange apparitions and everywhere Gogolian faces with thin noses, sharp-ending chins and small round eyes. When I came out, the night was dark blue and warm.

We went to see Patricia at the Opera House, trying to maintain a beautiful balance all by herself, while the rest of the cast were shouting, a burlesque performance, so that hers became slightly unbalanced, but she fought on, this exquisite light flowing out of her and an uncanny ability she has to give the illusion that she is floating above ground, the illusion of levitation.

We all went for supper afterwards, in the darkness of the restaurant, in the candlelights, her blue-green eyes were sparkling like gems full of fire.

NOVEMBER

Very hot suddenly, the light falling everywhere, the haze rising over the city and the strong wind sweeping the papers away.

Patrick White was at the awards presentation. His eyes full of an afternoon light and his face ascetic-looking. The mouth thin and mobile and full of sharpness, with a thin, lizard tongue.

He was tall, thinning, dressed in blue gray, interested in the groups, the people around him, already, one felt, dissecting them, his mouth and his face falling in a sort of disparaging expression and his eyes gleaming with some wickedness as he talked about the professor.

Very hot yesterday. Listening to the Haydn cello concerto on the radio, I thought it was Jacqueline du Pré playing. The tones burning with a youthful energy, as if the surface of the sound was touched with a sheet of fire, that explosiveness that comes with youth. But it was Rostropovich, in fact.

I think of him in more sombre tones. It must have been an earlier recording, or maybe Haydn has put it there, so that it comes alive when it is played.

Last night I was watering the plants on the terrace, birds were flying out of them. Finally I found and picked up this little sparrow, totally afraid and wet, making small noises, its feet clinging to my hand. I put it high on the tree. Later I found another one that had fallen from its nest.

The whole night the wetness of their feathers, their smell, the beating of their hearts, the aliveness of their bodies in my hand, their feet clinging to me brought the image of Mrs. Crawford, her thin hands that were picking the covers as if undoing them slowly, not enough strength to move them.

I had gone to see her at the nursing home. The place clean, full of Fijian, Islander nurses, large peaceful presences, at ease in their physicality.

Mrs. Crawford looked at me with clear blue eyes, the same color as her ring. This gurgling came from inside as if a singsong, the nurse said that she was trying to talk.

I could not see any recognition in her eyes. Her face looked well, free from all the complaints and unhappiness, as if released. Released, going out, smaller still in her mobile bed, pulling the covers with her thin hands, picking at them slowly, as if a bird, with smaller and smaller movements.

One of the sisters came and arranged the bed, her hair, totally white now, spoke to her, took her hand, said "Hold my hand."

Mrs. Crawford was holding it. The sister was pleased. She said, "She is squeezing my hand."

Mrs. Crawford seemed tired. I spoke of the house, friends, she was yawning, looking at me with great open blue eyes, as if trying to remember, to understand, totally locked in now in this absolute silence. She looked small, as if sitting in a cradle, her movements connected to some inner line that we were unaware of, maybe the people in the hospital who were used to this dialect.

It seemed as if she was already disappearing into the cave, the secret darkness from which this faint message was still coming.

Woke up suddenly in the middle of the night.

The city quiet. At the back of Harold Park the new building totally illuminated, hanging on to the dark sky like a lighted birdcage.

The sky blue green with the lighted building looking very delicate. The birds were just beginning to speak before sunrise.

In the crowded coffee shop at lunchtime. They were sharing my table, the little boy, Sasha, his mother and grandmother. When they brought him his milk, he found it too cold and complained, told the waitress to take it away.

His mother was pleading with him, "You can't do that Sasha."

When the sandwiches arrived, he was uncertain about them too.

"The beginning of taste," I said to the mother.

He was watching me with curiosity. Already a personality.

"You have a lovely name," I said to him. "Wear it well."

"Thank the lady, Sasha," said the mother.

Why should he thank me? I think he understood me. It is the grown-ups that always get in the way with all these superficial sociabilities.

DECEMBER

On the ABC a young, very lively-looking violinist playing Bruch's *Scottish Fantasy*, a sentimental but technically very good tone, full of surface energy, changing dresses to play Sarasate's arrangement of *Carmen*, short red dress, high boots. Finally, fully wired and with a white plastic-looking violin, playing some modern piece, jumping about the stage.

The orchestra, an elderly group of musicians, looking indulgently at this young puppy displaying herself, she motioning them to rise at the applause, everything not de rigueur at all, the conductor's role usurped at every stage, like a young upstart bent on utilizing power.

Looking at the crowds outside the milk bar at lunchtime. It is as if no one carries an inner life any longer, empty shells full of movement, action, action. No one wants to work at inner issues, a work which has been discredited.

Reading about Satie and Ravel. Ravel refusing the Légion d'honneur. And Satie: "It is not enough to refuse it. One should never have deserved it."

A picnic by the river, boats gliding up and down, orchards arranged geometrically like intricate French gardens, cows in the paddocks with black or brown shining skins as if made of silk, watching us.

Then we all went to the orchard, the silence of the evening flowing above the fir trees. Small, pretty-looking children chasing a black kitten, and the Italian, lean and sunburnt, talking of coming to live here away from the noise of the cities, he was in Ethiopia, with the army during the war, then to India and finally here.

The evening was falling softly in dark shadows, smells of lilies and onions, the sounds of cicadas and we, very pleased with our boxes of freshly picked fruit.

A program on television about life in the future with computers, cyberspace, changes to work patterns. People somehow left out of the picture. The clinical aspect of it all, the unreality.

They spoke of "talking to the world." What can that mean? These terrible abstractions that are meaningless in inner terms. The direction—everyone working from home with a computer and a phone, coming from time to time into an office painted in strong colors, everyone plugging immediately into a computer.

The program described the future as having "LIMITLESS POSSIBILITIES." They have obviously forgotten about the dark forces, our intrinsic limitations, a sort of empty naivety to the language.

A totally sterile business, out of communities, landscapes, relationships to places, to life, to human exchanges. TV Channel advertising their Saturday night entertainment: A thrilling night of TERROR and CRIME.

Reading Osip Mandelstam, his prose full of light, the weight well distributed, balancing itself. Masterful. The concentration, the exactness of impressions, of images. I was very moved.

His childhood impressions, simple lines, something upright about it, like an elegant, well-made chair, waiting in the room of the world.

Christmas day, on the terrace, the tree creaking in the wind, as I looked up, the long branches as if a ship on the sea of the sky, moving with a circular motion. The sun shining, from next door the scent of roast drifting in the wind together with Tom Lehrer singing:

> . . . Angels we have heard on high . . . tell us to go out
> and buy . . .

JOURNAL IX

TRAVEL

PARIS, FIRST VISIT—MAY

The light silver gray, the room in the old hotel dark, nothing has changed since my last visit. The double bed is still of brass and shimmering, the doors cast in medieval times, need two people to open them, the key, as if the key of the city of Paris, the narrow lift still rattling, puffing up. And down in the Rue Godot, the ladies of the night are still doing business, slightly more extravagantly dressed than I remember. One with blonde reddish hair and a brown jacket, with several rabbit furs hanging around her neck, like hunting trophies, all of them the most iridescent red browns. Her dog, a ginger color too.

Old ladies walk their dogs past the Sexashop sign.

I come out of the hotel immediately to look at the boulevards, La Madeleine, the Opera, the Galeries Lafayette, they are all still there, unchanged, and everywhere the sound of French . . . French . . .

The city full of buskers, the flute player in front of Lafayette, looking like Manet's *The Fifer.* A young handsome face, wearing a black beret, he was accompanied by a banjo player. Quick rhythms, well-articulated phrases, the music rising out of the street, into the sky, a flight that took us with him.

Yesterday, the cellist in the Metro. I had lost my way in the Underground when I came across him at the crossroads of two tunnels, in a narrow tiled corner. He was sitting on a stool, his coat was hanging from a rail. He was young, almost an adolescent, with black eyes and hair, the score was open in front of him, and he was drawing these long, full tones. Bach was reverberating in the closed space. And as I came up on the platform, the sound was coming through the pores of the concrete, through the openings, as if the earth was singing.

As always I am watching the shop windows with the natives. The sweets at Fauchon's—burnt caramel, delicate apricot, Degas's browns, off-whites, greens, like the sea that afternoon at Surfers Paradise, sea green, green in the sunlight, bottle green. Everything has a line, neat, well proportioned, the shops, the pavements. Honeys from all over the world, even from Romania, linden flower honey. And past La Madeleine, a fish shop, caviar, sea serpents, their skins the color of dark amber. The smell of cheeses in the Galeries Lafayette.

The service was on at La Madeleine. Originally built by Napoleon as a Temple of Glory to the soldiers of the Grande Armée. It became a Catholic church under the

Restoration. An imposing, heavy structure, enormous columns, a structure sustaining itself by sheer size. The lights like clusters of giant grapes, painted cupolas with fleshy saints, an organ with a bellowing voice.

But when the massive doors open at the end of the service and the light streams in from outside, a revelation somehow, the boulevard opening into the Place de la Concorde, the Seine, the dwarfed size of the people on the massive steps, as if one is watching an apocalyptic painting.

By comparison, Notre Dame seems spirit itself, resting at ease, the outside walls as if carved from the finest of ivory, the arches inside, soaring, creating a sense of space, of flight. The tones of the organ, an ancient, yet modern quality, sustaining the service.

I walked to the Louvre today. Along Rue de Rivoli tourist buses. It was Sunday, a free day, and the place was full of people. But in spite of this the palaces could cope well. The scale, the architecture, the ceilings. The ceilings everywhere in Paris have been a revelation. I am watching them avidly. Some are elegant and simple as at the Marigny Theater, with its gilded dome and the chandelier, a crown of delicate pearls. Others are baroque, overworked, but with a presence, opulent, as in the Louvre, and others, thinking of the moving lines of the arches in the medieval churches, La Sainte-Chapelle, Notre Dame, rising like the delicate ribs of a body ascending, toward an absolute, like Brancusi's birds, full of lightness.

Inside the Louvre confronted yet again with rooms and rooms of paintings. I like the early ones better, the Renaissance somehow inflated everything, but the early Italian,

French, Dutch, more sombre, nearer to the subject matter, more modest.

Large rooms full of Rubens, Davids, Ingres, all of them still painting Hellenistic subjects—*Paris and His Judgment, Achilles and the Visitors*. But more alive in the small portraits, even David, watching out of his slightly crooked eye, next to his Madame Recamier.

Napoleon again, the immense canvases by David, Ingres, Gros, romantic photographs of the "emperor." The details so exact, the shapes so photographic, of men, horses, women, dresses, jewelry, and the Coronation painting.

But the Niki of Samothraki, rising at the top of the long staircase, was insinuatingly breathtaking. One could not take one's eyes off her, one felt the wind in those great, outstretched wings, the impact on the body and the draped clothes. None of the photographs do it justice, both more intimate and more imposing than any of the reproductions.

Finally, I found the old theater where Edwige Feuillère was playing in a revival of Giraudoux's *La Folle de Chaillot*. The theater like a narrow cylinder, enclosing one from all sides, gilded ornaments, now chipped. I was alone on the very last tier, the floor torn, the red skin of the seats worn out, the stuffing coming through like tufts of discolored hair.

The curtain was red and on it was painted a bottle of Schweppes held by a black-gloved woman's hand and above it the legend: "Schweppes, le drink des gens raffinés."

The air smelt of dust, the boxes below me were only one seat deep, as if painted curtains in a make-believe theater.

When the play started, Giraudoux proved to be the same, choked with dust and sentimentality. His language, which we had to study, then seemingly full of vitality and pyrotechnics, had aged very badly. Only Feuillère tried valiantly to bring it to life. The program notes full of Jouvet's love and admiration for Giraudoux's plays.

The Alexandre Bridge, full of imposing columns and horses, and facing it, La Place des Invalides, a vast square, the wind was blowing hard and the little people could be seen, far away, going into the Hotel des Invalides.

In the courtyard of the Musée de l'Armée, cannons, tall as a person, taken by the French army in battles, green-black, but worked most meticulously with engravings, flowers, arabesques, heads of lions. The chapel dedicated to the fallen, and below Napoleon's remains. The narrow place crawling with tourists, locals, school children and their teachers. The young restless, their lively eyes glistening in the semi-darkness. The teachers explaining how ". . . the Emperor wanted his ashes to rest in France, with the French people that he loved so much." And on the wall, one could see the procession going to St. Helena, how they reached the place, and someone overcome with emotion, falls on his knees.

". . . and now we will all turn to the right, slowly and without pushing, as gently as we can . . ." and the angels will proceed toward this dream of grandeur that was Napoleon.

Above, under the immense golden dome, Napoleon's tomb surrounded by statues in white marble, urns bearing the names of his victories—Iena, Austerlitz . . .

A lovely spring day, the light rising like haze above the green trees in the Champs Élysées. I asked directions to the Petit Palais, but all the people out at 10 a.m. on a Sunday were tourists.

The fountains were playing in the Place de la Concorde, and at the Petit Palais the Parisians had arrived, elegantly dressed, to see the Cézanne retrospective. The very people who, at the time, had not accepted him, so that he retired to the country and doggedly worked out the relationship between himself and form.

The works, done in the last ten years of his life, were marvelous. His "nature morte," as if once he caught them they remained alive for ever. His apples, his portraits, a somber line, but a lot of solid light, as if he had gone into the heart of nature and remade it into his image, a new reality. A tone about the exhibition, a total lack of superfluity, so absolutely right, so immediate and so seemingly simple.

Walking down the Boulevard des Capucines to the Opera. The theater full of lights, candelabras blooming into white, transparent fruit, the wide staircase, the gilded ceiling. I seemed to be the first in the empty theater, except for the television people. Everything in red and gold, baroque carvings, the Chagall ceiling and below it the flower-like chandelier.

Slowly they were coming in. The place intimate in spite of its size, the balconies, the boxes, filling with dark, brooding, ancient European faces, rising like ghosts from literary pages. Revolutionaries with long beards, leaning out to see better, all pressed somehow in the controlled space. Suddenly, the second set of lights came down from the ceiling, powerfully on us, and the painted curtain lowered.

We were all watching each other with curiosity, the boxes above us a feeling as in a Daumier painting, the series of *Les Dimanches d'un Parisien*. The Parisians taking their baths, all these heads next to each other, taking the air.

Monteverdi's *L'Incoronazione di Poppea*. Produced with great care, a star cast—Gwyneth Jones, Ghiaurov, and John Vickers. Vocally rich, flowing. The costumes beautiful. Monteverdi full of finesse, and the music, still with that early music austerity, and a purity of line, that contrasted with the lascivious subject of the opera.

But the interval was more of an event that somehow overshadowed the performance. As if the theater itself burning with lights, its magnificent mirrors, the large glass doors facing the balcony and the boulevards, the theater itself had taken over. The chandeliers discreetly setting off the space, the architectural lines, and we too, as we walked along the grand foyer, we had suddenly transformed from small, mundane people to personages with rich pasts, our reflections in the mirrors totally changed from what we knew, the place giving us another dimension.

The woman who brings me breakfast every morning—croissant and hot chocolate—resembles my grandmother that I have never known. She is tall, as in the photographs with Mother, with light brown hair, Grandmother's cheekbones and deep-seated eyes. She has a diffident air as she comes in, as if intruding on a forbidden space, but she seems well disposed toward me.

Today, I lighted a candle at Notre Dame, in memory of my grandmother and all our dead. The church was rather empty, peaceful. I remembered coming here with Mavis in Easter Week. The church was packed. The central part full of people sitting on chairs, enormous movement in the aisles, and the organ was breathing these long, somber, apocalyptical sounds, music black and humid like the weather outside, soaring into the arches, and people kept coming in all the time, moving as if part of a secret ceremony, as if waiting for some imminent disaster, some revelation that was going to happen any minute.

PARIS, SECOND VISIT—SEPTEMBER

Arrived early afternoon, very hot milky light. The city as if exhausted with summer, with the heat. Suddenly very tired. Crowds everywhere, the same crowds as in London, something indistinguishable about crowds.

The hotel changed, redesigned interiors, smaller rooms. Across the street, on the third floor of the apartment, people were finishing work, going down the narrow street, then an immense quietness, unreal in a hotel in the middle of Paris.

I dreamt of Mother, she was lecturing on a platform. I was in the audience, embarrassed and afraid. I was watching my hands. She was talking of the importance of style, I don't remember the exact words, how one must work at one's style. I was pleased with her, that she was so good in public. She was fully dressed as in the photograph on the mantelpiece at home, her navy coat and her beret on.

Raining. In bookshops, beautiful editions of the classics. Looked for Australian books, only a translation of Keneally. I was hoping to find a biography of Celan, but found only *Biographie de jeunesse* by Israel Chalfen. His childhood and youth in Romania, up to the time he left for Vienna. How things develop, how the future waits for us silently, and then strikes violently.

Reading *Anna Akhmatova: A Poetic Pilgrimage* by Amanda Haight. "I am easy in my mind now," said Akhmatova to

Nadezhda Mandelstam in the sixties—"We have seen how durable poetry is."

Left to go to the Orangerie, posted cards, the rain coming down, cool, misty over the Place de la Concorde, those magnificent openings toward the Champs Élysées. Japanese tourists photographing themselves, highly dressed, black, the latest gear.

L'Orangerie an old, modest building, to suit the paintings inside. The Soutines good, quirky, tortured, uneasy, trying constantly to come out, to find a peaceful place, fighting the air, his portraits, large hands, awkwardly placed, as if uneasy spoons with which the sitter is trying to hold life.

But his colors, a surprising mastery, the boy in red, a marvelous composition, the red so alive, so rich, as if vibrating in front of your eyes.

Cézanne again, self-contained and at ease, his apples, luminous glowing, the portrait of his son, the weight and yet the lightness of the forms.

Thinking of Mother, Father, the hands, the faces of all these old men and women one sees in the street, eating alone in restaurants, the old man asleep in the Metro, reminded me of Father, his white hair, his sunken cheeks, and the white bristle on his chin.

Baudelaire and his *Tableaux Parisiens*, "Ruines! Ma famille!" And those lines that I read a long time ago and have stayed with me ever since:

> Les morts, les pauvres morts, ont de grandes douleurs,
> Et quand Octobre souffle, émondeur des vieux arbres,

Son vent mélancolique à l'entour de leurs marbres,
Certes, ils doivent trouver les vivants bien ingrats,
A dormir, comme ils font, chaudement dans leurs draps,
Tandis que, dévorés de noires songeries,
Sans compagnon de lit, sans bonnes causeries . . .

"The dead, the poor dead, suffer terribly, and when October comes pruning the old trees, blows its melancholy wind around their marble monuments, they must surely find the living very ungrateful, to sleep, as they do, warmly between their sheets, while they, eaten up with black dreams, with no bed companions, no cozy chats . . ."

At the Louvre. It was raining heavily on Pei's Pyramide. It looked slightly out of place against the old palaces. Inside, a monumental elegance, the resonance of voices as if in a railway station. They used the same warm color of stone to match the old buildings, but from inside the glass structure seems heavy, too much metal to sustain it. Armies of tourists everywhere.

All nations seem to sell their past and that of its artists. Thinking of all the works in galleries, museums, all these private individuals trying to survive, to work, almost always with great difficulty, that have now become synonymous with national culture.

Private gestures that have been totally appropriated, even their experiments, their attempts to express something, to find a style, have become public property. Everything printed, reproduced, and tourists, tourists everywhere, buying them, photographing them . . .

At the Musée d'Orsay, newly opened, waiting with the crowd to get in. The old railway station, everything in strong, clean lines. French technology of the nineteenth century. The bronze statues outside the entrance, massive Brunhildas, to be placed on top of buildings, to be seen from afar, all with their breasts out.

The structure itself appearing light because of its size. Everything well resolved inside by the Italian architect Gae Aulenti, the right solutions to the structure, an elegant blending of light and color. But after walking around for two hours, the lines become heavy. One is constantly conscious of the architecture. Downstairs, sculptures of unknown artists famous in their day. The Impressionists on the third level, but even for them, the space too totalitarian.

Outside a pianist and a clarinettist were playing. I stayed on the steps eating my roll and thinking of the moving, tragic sculpture of an old woman by Camille Claudel, remembering my first visit to the Gare d'Orsay, where Madeleine Renaud and Jean-Louis Barrault had built their theater.

One discovered Barrault after the extraordinary impact of his *Baptiste* in *Les Enfants du paradis*, the Carné film, his lyrical silence that spoke to us all in a language of gestures.

Then reading his book *Reflections on the Theatre*, his beginnings—Dullin, Artaud, discussions about the actor, the authors, a person totally committed to the theater, searching for new possibilities, inclusiveness, working with actors, directors, writers, trying to survive as a theater company.

Discussing the *Compagnie Renaud-Barrault* he said: "Since 1947, that most rare, most noble, most deserving, the most difficult, to survive, I mean to be able to survive without selling yourself."

The entrance then was from the Quai d'Orsay. The two theaters had been built inside the railway station, they had space, functionality, and boldness of line. The downstairs theater was in the round, big and yet intimate. The focus of attention, two tree trunks in the middle that radiated to the ceiling and sustained the whole stage mechanism. Powerful, warm wood, like the spine of an animal that held us and the theater in its dynamic grasp.

I was enthusiastic about everything, the colors, the feeling of the place, a place where people worked, were aware of the past, but who knew that they had to prove themselves continuously.

Outside, in the foyer, the walls were full of posters, photographs of past performances, of actors, directors, writers, and in Barrault's handwriting a "thank-you note" to the architects, engineers, heads of construction, carpenters, electricians . . . who had worked to make the theater possible. Warm blood was circulating through the entire structure. The long list of their names, enlarged on the walls. It was the first time that I had seen this public inclusiveness, a desire to be part of a community, in the widest possible sense.

The foyer upstairs was empty, through the large windows one watched the Seine, the walls were painted with a fireplace, a mantelpiece with silver objects, tables . . . The only furniture was a large, white elaborate cage with two turtledoves, their cooing made the space homely.

The plays—Barrault in Nietzsche's *Thus Spoke Zarathustra*—presented as a fable, splendidly mounted, projections of images, singing, music by Boulez, the eagle, the serpent, the cows, the sun, the moon, masked characters in the story. All in Barrault's conception of "total theater."

Madeleine Renaud was appearing in *Harold and Maude*. She looked extremely light, fragile, warm and believable in the role, in the slightly improbable story of a very young man falling in love with an elderly woman. In the scene where both of them are bicycling in the forest, suddenly the theater filled with the image of a forest, trees on the walls, birds, the sun filtering on us through the green, we were in the middle of a forest, totally stunned by the effects of the cyclorama.

When I came out, the night was still and warm. I walked back to the hotel, the lights were blooming on the bridges, burning with a sustained light. I felt at home, a home that I had known for years, but had not seen. The river was full of reflections, the Louvre, the Tuileries Gardens on the other side, and over the bridge one could see another lighted bridge, and yet another, and Notre Dame rising softly in the distance.

PRAGUE—APRIL

The City

Night. With Alexandra in the Old Town Square, the place empty. The Town Hall, the famous Astronomical Clock, the massive Hus Monument, and above them all, the Tyn Church, its body and spires rising as if medieval knights in armor, metallic silver, a fantastic apparition in the night sky.

Alexandra walks fast in the narrow, intimate lanes, in her elegant black leather coat, her blonde hair flowing, keen to show me some historic coffee house where the revolutionaries met. She is pleased to be in her city.

In the daytime, the city, a soft presence in pastel colors. Not much space, but a constant intention of allowing it to breathe, to appear spacious. Excessive decorations on the buildings, statues of saints riding high above the spires surrounded by golden filigree auras, yet everything seems at ease, the extravagance absorbed by an underlying sombreness.

The Prague Writers' Festival (dedicated to Bohumil Hrabal)
The festival is being held in the Franz Kafka Center in the Old Town Square. Photographs of Kafka everywhere, as a child, an adolescent with thin legs, the young man looking at us with his dark, serious eyes. The women in his life.

At another level, the Milena Café. We eat and drink Bohemian wine, at the next table a woman with the profile of Nijinsky.

Groups of young Americans and their minders are having lunch. I am telling Alexandra that all men in Prague look either like Dvorak or like Havel.

Vera, Alexandra's mother, invites us for lunch in her apartment. A fifties building in the communist architectural style. She looks well, is pleased to see me, old friends from her earlier visit to Australia. The apartment is large, full of light and books. A professional translator, she discusses the new, rather changed situation. Before, they were translating the classics, but now, mostly massive new-age novels.

The Readings
Lawrence Ferlinghetti is the first reader. His impact on the Czech literary scene amazing, he is treated as if a rock star.

At the Lucerna Building, the previous day, long queues of young and middle-aged people waiting with their books to be signed by him. His early books as well, that they had bought during the short-lived liberation of the Prague Spring. He takes all this adulation modestly. In his interview with Michael March, the organizer of the festival, he speaks as a person engaged with life, everyday anecdotes about his famous friends, Ginsberg's funeral . . .

I am waiting on the bench for my turn to come, with Josef Topol, the very well known Czech poet and playwright, who will read after me. I am very nervous, as I usually am before a reading. He talks to me kindly, his entire attitude one of encouragement.

The hall is intimate and filled to capacity. Through the open windows one can see the top of the Old Town Hall. After I read I am so relieved inwardly and preoccupied that I hardly hear Topol, even though I am listening attentively to him.

All readings are multilingual. The largest group of writers is from Europe—Austria, Britain, Hungary, Italy, Portugal, Poland. As usual too much to absorb. One becomes more engaged with poets one has read before, in the Penguin Anthology *Child of Europe*, for instance.

The Polish poet Ryszard Krynicki, a handsome, elegant tall man, dressed in light gray, his head, his face as if illuminated from inside. His poetry has the same feeling.

And then Gyorgy Petri, the Hungarian dissident poet. He has come with a minder. But he reads well, listens attentively to the other readers, his face marked by age, even though only in his fifties. I think of Cavafy and his poem about the old poet:

. . . exhausted and bent
crippled by years and by excesses . . .

His poetry very strong, bold, sometimes savage. His poem "Electra," included in the festival program, sums up his style:

Because of disgust, because it all sticks in my craw,
Revenge has become my dream and my daily bread.
And this revulsion is stronger than the gods.
I already see how mould is creeping across Mycenae
Which is the mould of madness and destruction.

Outside the Kafka Centre life goes on, tourists everywhere, waiting in the Square to see the clock perform. Photographers, pointing their long lenses at us, apologizing, asking for permission. Ivan Kutak taking photographs of us at the opening of the Festival in the Old Town Hall, in front of the massive historic painting of Hus and his confrontation with the Catholic Church, one assumes.

Then the Italian photographer Rossano Maniscalchi, with his beautiful partner Asola, moving fast, trying to engage you, animate your face, photograph you unaware of being photographed.

Finally at the Kafka Bookshop for the launch of the two translated books, published by Marie and her One Woman Press. Marie, a tall young woman with beautiful cheekbones, a short punk haircut, dyed yellow, the same feeling of lightness in her movements and her English. Her husband, Miroslav, a gentle brooding face, arrives with their dog Barca, carried in a special bag.

The two books—*Absence*, translated by Alexandra, and Rhea Galanaki's *Albeit Pleasing*, translated from the Greek by Claudine, look small and elegant.

Rhea Galanaki, with her long, rich, curly red hair, has a direct almost fierce manner, which softens when she speaks. She is at the festival with her husband and her daughter Kyveli, a bright, precocious child, constantly testing my knowledge of Australian geography. "Which is the longest Australian river? The highest mountain?" Questions, which of course, I cannot answer, as we walk across the Charles Bridge, the magic of the night around us, the river, the illuminated buildings, the castle, the black statues above us, people walking, talking, couples kissing, to reach the other side of the river and the old palace, with its gardens full of tulips in bloom and under the trees a mysterious darkness.

The Castle

A feeling of light elegance under the warm April sun. A fountain, young guards in colorful uniforms, a Romanesque church with a red dusted façade, the Golden Lane with miniature houses painted in bright colors, where Kafka had a studio for a short time. Crowds of tourists filling the small interiors, buying . . . buying . . .

St. Vitus Cathedral, a tall, imposing Gothic structure, built over many centuries, so the guide tells us. Inside, the sheer height of the nave, chapels, stone busts, the relics of saints, stained-glass windows, an overwhelming richness of details, giving the place a dark extravagance.

When we come out, the light seems very strong.

For years the only association I had with St. Vitus was Rilke, and his *Notebooks of Malte Laurids Brigge*, that astonishing description of a man suffering from St Vitus Dance, walking down the Boulevard Saint-Michel in Paris.

The story begins with Malte coming out of his room feeling better, he is going to the Bibliothèque Nationale to read "his poet."

The boulevard is vast and empty. High up, the louvered windows are being opened with a clear sound of glass, their reflections flying like white birds above the street. Then a carriage passes, horses trotting, the restaurants are opening, tables are being set out by waiters, when suddenly, a group of them stop to watch something on the other side of the street and laugh. "I felt a fear growing in me," Malte tells us. "Something pushed me to cross the street."

He tries to find the object of this merriment, but he can see nothing in front of him except this tall, emaciated man in a dark coat, with a black soft hat resting on his faded blond hair. He has already decided that there is nothing laughable about the man, when suddenly something makes him stumble.

"I was following him closely. I was on my guard as I approached the spot . . . but there was nothing there." Slowly he discovers all the small involuntary jumps, the agitated movements of his hands, the terrifying struggle of the man to keep control of these convulsions. "From that moment on," Malte tells us, "I was tied to him."

He feels that this trembling travels through the man's body and tries to escape, here or there. He understands the fear the man has of the people in the street, and he begins to observe prudently if the passers-by notice anything. He asks himself how he can come to the man's aid.

The convulsions had now reached the collarbone, the man was trying to stop them with his walking stick. Malte was following him closely, offering him inwardly his own strength, hoping that the man will use it.

But as they reached the Place Saint-Michel, everything broke out of him:

". . . the stick had disappeared, he spread his arms as if he wanted to fly, and this burst out of him like a force of nature, bent him forward, pushed him violently backward . . . and like a sling threw its wild dance into the crowd . . . for a lot of people had gathered and I could see him no longer . . ."

"I could continue on my way," Malte tells us, "but what was the point? I felt empty. Empty like a piece of paper drifting aimlessly along the houses on the boulevard . . ."

Walks in the City

A soft rain was falling in the morning, but by the time we set out with Esther to visit Josefov, it had stopped.

The ancient Jewish Cemetery, melancholy in the wet light, the trees still wintery. The tombs fenced in by massive apartment blocks. The heavy tombstones with Hebrew writing, washed out, seemed as if events had compacted them, pulled them close together, bent them. In the guide book, we are being told, the Hebrew name for the Cemetery is: Beth Chaim, meaning "The House of Life."

The Old Synagogue in simple, modest lines, the earliest Gothic building in Prague, began in the eleventh century. In the middle an elaborate black wrought-iron cage, from which, one assumed, the Torah would have been read. The delicate chandeliers coming down to light the rather dark interior.

Past the Cemetery, buildings that now house an exhibition of drawings from the Jewish Ghetto in Terezin, among them naive drawings by children, who later perished in the camps. Then the Memorial Hall in the Pinkas Synagogue, for the Czech and Slovak Jews who perished, the walls covered with carved stone lists of their names.

Late afternoon, walking uphill for yet another celebration of the festival, the old streets, houses with rich architectural details, on the green hills, the trees were coming into bloom. From above, a moving youthful white, as if a valley of snowed trees.

With Alexandra to Prague Radio. A young, polite, softly spoken Vladimira to conduct the interview. The building, a fifties structure. Corridors, corridors, voices, small rooms, tables full of accumulated objects as if coming out of Svankmajer's film—Alice in Wonderland. The lift has no doors, one has to jump in and out, a series of boxes in perpetual motion. Maybe Svankmajer had designed the lift too.

Walking in the city this morning, I discovered a plaque on the wall of a building, and above it, in a niche, the bronze bust of a young woman. A very unusual occurrence, women seldom make it in bronze on city walls.

Bozena Nemkova, the plaque said, 1829–1862. I imagined her to be a revolutionary, but later, reading Peter Demetz's book—*Prague in Black and Gold*—discovered that she was a writer.

"Her novel—*The Grandmother* (*Babicka*)—written in 1855, is considered the first novel of the modern Czech tradition. A book that for 100 years has been fundamental to the Czech prose canon."

The bronze face is of a young, handsome woman, with a rather resigned, melancholy look. Peter Demetz, quoting historical sources says that "her friends and enemies, speak of her raven-black hair of metallic luster, dark eyes under strong brows and a high seriousness of feeling.

"A passionate woman who died young. *The Grandmother* written at a time of despair and misery recalls the idyllic days of her childhood, at home, in north-eastern Bohemia, and the old woman closest to her heart . . . the life of her grandmother, symbolic of strong vitality and loving wisdom."

JOURNAL X

JANUARY

A fine rain and very humid. Late afternoon it cleared totally, blue sky, a slight wind and at night a brilliant, full round moon. It disappeared slowly behind some clouds, apricot-pink light, then nothing, just a glow behind the clouds that seemed to suffuse them, slightly off the bridge.

Annoyed with life somehow. Turned on the radio. Listeners' requests on the ABC, suddenly Lipatti playing Bach's *Keyboard Concerto* arranged by Busoni. A 1949 transmission, amazing dark, warm tones, beautiful articulated fast passages, the orchestra too sounding real, without the current gloss of recordings in which the tones somehow disappear to leave this gooey substance as if achieved by a mixer . . . an immediacy to the playing. I felt better, in an optimistic mood.

In the restaurant for Indra's birthday. The walls full of graffiti, the management encouraging everyone to write something on the walls. Above our table someone had written: "Oedipus, ring your mother."

Toward morning dreamt of Max. Small and shrouded in white as if a mummy, his head and his face also bandaged, only his eyes were alive looking at me wistfully, he was stretching in a bed, his hind legs and his tail coming out of the shroud.

I felt very sad.

Last night a documentary on Kerouac, his style alive, full of something Whitmanesque, in prose. A poetry of the everyday, with these tendencies to rise toward something magnificent, speaking of the country as if it were alive, in its vastness.

Definitely a nakedness about him that one does not see in other writers, self-destruction, as well, inability to cope with fame.

His writer friends around him very articulate, speaking a direct and subtle language at times—Corso, Ferlinghetti, McLaren, Ginsberg. As well as a lot of self-indulgence, American hype, the land, as here, a vastness that always forces large gestures, unsustainable, that ultimately become empty.

Ginsberg saying that Kerouac trained like an athlete before starting to write. But we all try to help this inner process by constantly making space for it, more and more space, so that finally our lives are hollowed out and all the space is taken to produce these few lines.

Dinner at Franco's. His cooking always a touch of opulence, especially the colors, like his paintings, subtle colors, as in his last exhibition, yellows, yellows, reds . . . vibrating in their combinations, floating, rising out of their abstractions to meet you halfway. A refined, lyrical line.

Tonight, his soup a magnificent dark red tomato, rich, and on top, a slice of crushed carrot and spinach, the most amazing combination.

FEBRUARY

At night the view was spectacular, the sea moving from far away toward us, full of lights, people noise, sea spray. We were discussing Ola, her recent death, how much they had liked her. They intended to call on her in Adelaide, stay with her maybe, she had invited them the last time she was here.

Thinking of her I realized how environments form us, and then changing them, all these European landmarks that totally lose their meaning in another culture, personalities we were brought up with, writers that have no resonance at all in this culture, no one knows these things except us, a secret knowledge meaningless to people outside the old culture. And all this illusion of universalities, internationalism.

Death
As if pruning
Nearer to us
Then further out
Then back closer . . .

Looking at the young in town, the young will never know how lovely they look.

She was back in Australia for the ceremony. She still looked at Australian society with affection and contempt, like the young. She was saying that she went away to escape her parents, find herself, but now that they were both gone there was no reason for staying away. But she had a life elsewhere.

When she spoke about someone she disliked, her entire face collapsed, but her eyes dark and very warm, thinking from inside, trying to come to some balance.

Lloyd Rees talking about his life, his work: "Our lives, this miracle of living in the midst of endlessness."

A rerun of the old Monty Python Flying Circus, one of the actors dressed in a mad costume announcing: "Sexual ecstasy is overrated."

Maybe we should send this message to all this light pornography that surrounds us on television, magazines, papers.

I planted the new tree in a bigger pot, put it in the small garden at the back, it is as if a new person has arrived in one's intimacy. An adjustment, in the space, the other plants.

At the Yarra Club at La Perouse, beautiful evening over the sea, the planes landing far away, silently, the sun sinking into the sea in magnificent colors.

A quiet, nice evening on the veranda, eating fish and chips, drinking shandies, being bitten by mosquitos.

We were at the new gallery for the opening. Someone was playing the grand piano and waiters were offering sushi and drinks. The audience was discussing the pedigree of the furniture, the important provenance of the couch, the mirrors. The paintings were being watched at close range by collectors with harsh faces.

MARCH

In the dream I was discussing with a group of friends the question of poetry readings . . . I was saying, the moment you stand up to read, there is a sudden shock being registered by the body. All right, I was saying, you have made it, you are standing in front of an audience without falling down. Then I was expanding some very profound insights, but the only thing I remembered when I woke up was the question of tempo. The feeling from inside that things are moving very slowly, that you should read faster, while in actuality you are reading very fast . . . some alteration of time.

The ABC showing a repeat of the Cartier-Bresson documentary, in his eighties, he went back to drawing, his first love. He referred to drawing as a meditation. He was quoting Cioran: "Death does not make appointments." Then Cocteau: "Celebrity is good if you are unknown."

Rereading Bulgakov's *The Master and Margarita*, very well sustained, a human, yet terrible and cutting irony. The Devil, always well dressed, with good manners on the surface, always bringing foods of an exotic kind, in Russia at that time, when it was difficult to have either good clothes, food or space, he always has large apartments, suddenly creates a mirage of space.

The whole thing so well sustained, taking you in, his dialogue, the freedom of his scenes as if totally cleared of any encumbrances.

Greek proverb: The world has no handles for one man to walk off with it over his shoulders.

Read Imre Kertész's *Kaddish for an Unborn Child.* Human, in touch with deeper realities, at the same time, stylistically obsessive, circular movements to the prose, like a vortex into which he takes you, brings you out, takes you in again. Some irony, a conversation with oneself, a conversation with the reader. I liked him.

War. War everywhere. A general referring to one of the planes that saw "a window of opportunity" and dropped some bombs. The euphemisms they are using.

Watching again some analysis of the Second World War—Nazis, Communists, and so on.

Essentially—*abuse*—in all its forms destabilises intrinsically a person, a relationship, a society, a nation, the world. Yet the only way in which they feel this balance can be redressed is violence. But violence changes the nature of the redressing. Unbalances everything again.

APRIL

I went out for a walk, down Parramatta Road, large Italian shops full of Italian objects, marvelous glass—glasses, bottles, vases, bowls, enormously delicate or very fancy, like echoes of past tastes, of a finesse unseen nowadays, of lives, intimacies that we see in film, but not as an everyday happening.

Westpac in the meantime are pursuing me with their "Accidental Death Insurance." This is the third time they are sending it to me. I must tell them, for us superstitious people, this is a bad omen.

Raining, the trees moving in the wind their wet feathers. On the electricity line, the dance of the birds, these two pigeons the most acrobatic dance in the rain that was falling, taking a bath, exposing their bellies, underarms, top feathers, fanning them out in the most magnificent gliding, slow motion. The soft, gray rain kept falling on them, while they slipped from their precarious positions and righted themselves again, in some other way, to expose another part of their bodies.

Silent, gray gyrations on the electricity line.

The atmosphere in the pub, groups of men talking to each other inside that closed, dark structure, as if enclosed in a warm incubator, their voices rising edged with the violence of drink, a sudden, unnatural freeing of their voices so that the level was menacing, artificial, unrelated to them.

Sibelius being quoted in a documentary: "The terrifying creatures of the eternal silence."

La Cenerentola at the Opera House, Rossini full of brio, vivacity with an at-ease light touch. Witty, fast.

When we came out the city was rising lighted in the mist, massive shapes floating above the ground.

Meeting Sarah at the casino for lunch, Boyd would have had an apoplectic attack to see all that color, lights flashing everywhere in the semidarkness. Floral carpets, machines clicking away, things hanging from the ceiling, a nightmarish sort of place full of people moving in the semidarkness, large cars being exhibited, fish in giant aquariums . . .

Reading Elizabeth Hardwick's *Seduction and Betrayal*, a series of essays on women writers. An incisive style, irony, no sentimentality, stress on the heroism of work, persistence with writing, the assertion of some women writers in the face of social difficulties. Wide-ranging essays looking at novels, most of the heroines killed off. As Akhmatova used to say of Tolstoy's heroines: "Biology is destiny only for women."

The days marvelous, the air crisp and the sun clean, autumn resonance in the air, the blue of the sky pouring down.

MAY

This time last year we were in Kakadu National Park gliding silently on Yellow Water, the Alligator River in the early morning, the sun rising, crocodiles coming up to sun themselves on the banks, waterlilies opening, gum trees, their roots, their trunks in the water, their reflections full of strange effects, as if watching a ghost forest. Jesus birds walking on top of the water, their heads with red caps, picking at the vegetation after the wet.

Pandanus. Everyone busy photographing. As we advanced, the boat very silent, openings that looked as if architecturally designed by water gardeners, the waves of the boat, sculpted on the surface.

Then Nourlangie Rock, a noble outcrop, imposing. Tall grass, blond silver trees, ethereal, moving in the wind. Black wattle, the real feeling of sacred sites, some lived yet aloof quality about them.

Inside, dark red stone walls, overhanging galleries, a friendly wind blowing through them, the sunlight filtered through narrow openings, high, as if cathedral heights. The walls rich with paintings of kangaroos, dancers, gods, the first people—energy and movement.

Very hot outside the galleries. We stopped at the Anbangbang billabong for lunch. A green lake covered in waterlilies, some opening, moving white-mauve from afar. Gums everywhere, a pair of hawks, brown green, a delicate dove, silver pink gray and a crow with a harsh voice and feathers of a magnificent brilliant black, our only companions.

As we ate we threw small pieces of bread and cheese on the ground, the ground full of the debris of retreating waters. The hawks were diving with beautiful precision, picking up the pieces, missing, dive-bombing again, wings outstretched, as if high-flyers, athletes practicing a move, again and again. The dove after them on the ground, delicate and somehow fearful, with its elegant turquoise head and neck, as if wearing Egyptian necklaces. But the hawks angry with the crow, muttering darkly when it came on their tree.

At night, after dinner, we wrote cards at the long wooden table. "Greetings from the Top End. Beautiful places, crocodiles and waterlilies. Solitary places and noble outcrops, Aboriginal paintings, distances and heat. We took to them as if our natural element . . ."

Driving and driving to Tennant Creek. Miles and miles of totally open country, flat horizons, blond grass, red soil, giant ants' nests.

We stopped for lunch in the bush. Under some trees two brolgas on their thin legs, silver white feathers. When they opened their wings a vision of red, they beat the air with them as they retreated from us.

I remembered the first time I saw the Brolga Dance, performed by a very young David Gulpilil, the gracefulness of the movements, the sound of the sticks, the sudden cries, the transformation of the body, so that you almost saw the bird in movement.

Discussions over lunch—Europe, parents, attitudes in the thirties, forties. Mother, when young, with her socialist tendencies. After marriage, at home, discussing politics, agrarian reforms in Romania, and so on.

In Tennant Creek dinner at the RSL. While getting our food I asked the girl serving not to put sauce on my meat and to give me another serving of potatoes instead of cauliflower. She could not cope with this departure from the norm, put sauce on it, was offering it to Jurgis, asking him if he wants "A NORMAL ROAST."

After dinner we drove through town, very dark, everything closed, only the figures under the trees, walking, silent, moving imperceptibly somehow. It seemed that when the whites went home, they came out to claim their country back.

In the morning we traveled to The Pebbles, women's ceremonies place. Under the sharp blue sky, small outcrops looking like breasts coming out of the soft, blond grass, and further out—The Devils Marbles—*Karlwekarlwe Karlu Karlu*—The Sacred Meeting Place.

A city of giant stones listening in the silence. The soil, brick red and the plants transparent and very delicate, but dry. Very hot, a slight breeze, the light, glyka, sweetness, as the Greeks would say.

The Aboriginal legend of the Marbles is that the people who created them live in caves, underground. Children who are coming to play there are attracted by them, taken underground, kept there. Dangerous and powerful forces difficult to resist.

We walked around, the landscape deceptive, easy to get lost, among these massive red shapes balancing on top of each other. On the little hills, heavy formation like sculptures by Moore. Birut had seen them at night, with the moonlight on them, a wondrous landscape, powerful and frightening at the same time.

The country everywhere full of deeper meanings, cosmic fears, myths, spirits, the creators, the first people, the rainbow serpent, totems. It seemed that only the Aboriginal people were bringing a metaphysical dimension to the landscape, for the rest of us, technology, and the idea of instant access to things, inner training no longer a necessity—instant religion, instant art and so on.

As we came out of town, the sky dusted blue and full of floating clouds. The trees with their thin, black bodies, a formation against the sky that made them look like brolgas, or in the distance, with their round canopies, the look of trees in Italian Renaissance religious paintings.

Dream in the little motel in Angathella: it seemed that we had arrived at this very large house at dusk. Glass doors overlooking a garden. It seemed that we were in need of a lawyer. Someone had gone to find one. Then they arrived.

When I went up the steps inside the lounge room a priest was there in full robes, carrying an incense burner. The room full of men in black. Lawyers or undertakers?

On a raised platform they had placed two large objects looking like coffins, but when I approached they were two carved figures, one in dark, red wood, the Aboriginal colors, the other covered in golden white paint. Totemic figures for some ceremonial performance.

I was astonished at all this. I thought that the house was new and they had brought the priest to bless it. Mother suddenly appeared and kissed the hand of the priest. A very unusual gesture for her, I never remember her doing it. I somehow followed, kissing the edge of his sleeve which had a rough texture.

In a second they had all disappeared. We were in the empty lounge room discussing lawyers, travel, advertising brochures with photographs of motorcyclists with helmets on, as we had seen on the road, that always remind me of Cocteau's "angels of death."

In Winton, at the Caravan Park, we went to a dinner performance by the local bush poet—Gloria—a tall lady in red trousers and a large hat full of badges. We waited on chairs around the fire, we were offered curry stew and damper, together with bush poems and rather heavy jokes. As we left, the sky still, and the new moon, delicate, just a thin slice on the white transparent shade of the moon.

When we came back, Sydney wet and humid. I kept on traveling at high speed, especially when lying in bed. A kind of levitation. When I woke up at night, the feeling of being in a glass bubble of light, empty golden landscapes, a muted light coming through the windows, everywhere.

JUNE

Dream. It seemed that the Japanese were conducting research into traffic problems. Then the view of a highway with cars passing at speed, and between them, rolling with the same speed, human heads that had been cut off precisely at the neck, so that you could see the hollow entry to the head and the nerves around the skin. The heads rolled on as if propelled by some inner speed trying to match the cars.

Looking at a production of Bartok's *Bluebeard's Castle* on television. Very powerful, strange, dramatic effects. The lake of tears in the castle. I remembered Simon Rattle saying that Bartok had difficulties establishing an intimate relationship with a woman, the lake of tears forbidding the woman's approach.

In the Canadian production an immense sadness, the tragedy too of the women kept in these inner cages in static positions, unable to move, to love. At least this is how the director of the production had seen it. I don't know what Bartok's actual directions are.

But what a struggle he had to survive, to compose, many compositions not performed at all, not liked either. His face in the photographs very tragic, and then leukemia. And now they have moved his body with great pomp and reburied it in Hungary. The irony of all this.

Handel at the Opera House—*Giulio Cesare*—a marvelous performance with Yvonne Kenny and Graham Pushee. The music elegant, moving, full of youthful enthusiasm, uplifting, and the voices were constantly taking off, flying in an effortless movement, upward.

A very simple, effective and intelligent production, always in harmony with the music and the spirit of the opera, subtle in its effects, by Francisco Negri.

In the interval, the view from inside, Sydney through the glass, the bridge looking well balanced, the lights, the ferries passing. A magic place, I said to Warwick, always taking one by surprise.

JULY

The sun has come out and the city is steaming in the light. Fog this morning, we are totally covered in fog.

Thinking of Bachmann:

Fog land I have seen
Fog heart I have eaten . . .

Very early morning, in the dark house, feeling sad, nothing left now but objects. When we go, the objects will remain in the house, still here, unaware of our passing.

I thought of the beautiful, old Russian dancer being interviewed. A friend, another dancer, was asking her:

"Nina, do you remember the sable coat you were wearing at the time?"

And Nina:

"But does the sable coat remember me?"

In the Ivory Coast film, the miracles and excesses of religion. This man, the new prophet, wants to prove to the people that he is immortal. He brings someone to shoot him so that he can prove that bullets don't harm him. He dies.

A lesson for all these religious fanatics, but the ones around us don't submit themselves to such tests, unfortunately, and go on claiming immortality without any proof.

How curious it is reading Pavese's journals *Le Métier de vivre*. You have no inkling of what was really going on inside him. This constant transformation, this hiding of what we feel or fear into analytical thought, comparative points, literary analogies and so on. I assume to diminish the potency of events. It is as if you are reading of a parallel person to Pavese.

Giacometti: "What is important is to create an object capable of conveying a sensation as close as possible to the one felt at the sight of the subject."

Culling letters, papers, again and again, so much excessive material. But it all seems difficult, as if the material too has its own periphery of existence and resents being denied its space.

We went to see Antonio in his new studio. Good, disciplined performances. This "austere flamboyance" that is flamenco, these guttural voices that cry, like rembetika. A flamenco singer from Spain was there, crying out in these rugged tones, fighting an imaginary bull with a red scarf, the constant use of the body as an instrument, with minimal technical additions, clapping one's hands, hitting the body for sound, the whole body as a resonating chamber.

AUGUST

Simón Bolívar talking of his life, before he died at forty-seven: "After twenty years of struggle I have come to realize that I have been ploughing the sea."

Listening to the concert on the ABC, the applause came like a rapid, persistent rain.

All these funerals! All these funerals! In the same crematorium, each time in another chapel, or the same one. The same shrubs, flowers, little statues, groups of people that had not seen each other for a long time, brought together by this final event. Sociabilities. Religion trying to fill these terrible gaps, telling us of after life, the love of God, the Lord's Prayer.

Then coming out in the cold wind, crying a little, more sociabilities, cups of tea, sandwiches, cakes, talking in subdued voices. The family going home. All that effort of looking after someone now an empty space.

On Saturday afternoons they all drove around the city to look at houses, cars, objects, mechanical objects, a repetition of objects, whose mythology had been built through advertisements, but which finally brought little to one's life.

A direction in which the actual desire was the element, a suspended desire that brought them all out to gaze at cars that stood newly polished and heavy resting under the brilliantly colored paper streamers blowing in the breeze.

The space had been cut from the fields, transformed into concrete floors, sad and unplaced beside the highway, naked of trees, where the small, earlier houses had stood. Now they were left to crumble, black with soot and abandoned.

An article in an old *Times Literary Supplement*, by Karen Thomas, on the *Rigveda*, an anthology of over a thousand songs, written long before Homer's poems, in an earlier form of Sanskrit. They translated one of the poems, "To the Breath of the Gods":

> May the wind blow healing hither
> Kind, refreshing to us in the heart
> May it extend our lives.
>
> Wind, you are to us a father
> And a brother and our friend
> So equip us for life.
>
> And if, Wind, there in your house
> A store of immortality is laid,
> Give some to us that we may live.

SEPTEMBER

Hot today, spring as usual an unsettling element. The gum tree is shedding its leaves, these marvelous warm colors all over the lawn, full of scent.

How she is trying to write about her mother. She did not like her, a woman not fit to be a mother, neurotic, cruel. She always used to romanticize her, but when she finally went into this feeling of guilt about her, writing about it, she said, does not liberate you, nor solve any issues.

I agreed. A dangerous activity as well. Bringing these inner elements into the sharp focus required to write about them proves to be explosive in inner terms, and then they remain more defined in you, which makes things more difficult.

The critics were discussing Kafka. Trying to catch this animal, his writing, force it into some shape, some straight disciplined lines.

He was saying that his work will not survive. He is still painting with a brush on small-scale canvases. He is not taking risks.

But what does taking risks mean? These are critical terms used by people to appraise works in retrospect. At the moment of work one is working only with something to be expressed and trying to find the adequate stylistic means to bring it out, give it life, make is remain alive, if possible.

Taking risks sounds like a business consultant's vocabulary.

In the Gershwin documentary, Virgil Thompson giving us his not-very-approving views on Gershwin. Virgil—a slow, elderly, rather acrid man.

Very beautiful, fragile weather, the trees in bloom, birds running about with their spring duties, the scent of jasmine in the air.

But the HUMANS—a terrible race . . . more and more disasters, shootings, killings, the Press feeding this type of approach, reading more and more about disasters, crying, deaths, we are becoming more and more voyeuristic, everyone praying, praying everywhere, but this does not seem to change anything, the killings go on.

We have to say with Madame de Sévigné: "The more I see of men, the more I admire dogs."

OCTOBER

Spring winds always remind me of Lavrion. The same winds hot and dusty, full of sand from the beach, that used to affect my eyes. The powerful uneasiness in our lives in the camp. The Commission had arrived. We waited in the corridors upstairs, would we manage to leave this time?

This type of fear, a twentieth-century fear, everyone writing about it, experiencing it.

On the radio, on TV, the strangulated-with-excitement voices of sports commentators.

Spirituals on television with Jessye Norman and Kathleen Battle, their voices like birds in flight, beautiful to watch and hear, enormous musicality, movement, nuances and the songs amazing in their simplicity and yet complexity of rhythms, tempos, very difficult to perform, a sort of Rossini vocalizations.

Levine conducting very sympathetically. The immediacy, the simplicity of the storytelling, as if an alive story, that had just happened . . .

"Well, Jesus said . . ." as if he were here, in the street.

Carnegie Hall full, it took them more than a hundred years to gain some legitimacy for the form. The choir at the back, sombre in their dark-blue and red gowns.

The weekend very pleasant but silent. Very hot as if summer, the house closed with drawn curtains, and outside, the light massive over the city.

The spring wind, the grandmother going down the street pushing a pram, the child moving its legs in the rhythm of the pram, a black bird landing on the tree with a heavy sound, opening its wings, splashing the air with a black sound, and I talking to Mother: "What is this, do you think, spring paralysis?"

The roses already in bloom.

At the cemetery by bus, a long trip, through the dusty rundown suburbs. The cemetery empty in the midday sun, a whitewashed wind blowing and the city sinking in the blue gray mist.

Very hot. The wind smelling of smoke. From time to time, far away a woman bending over a grave, the lettering already fading from the tombstones.

NOVEMBER

Last night on SBS—*A Day in the Life of Tarkovsky*.

The filming of *Sacrifice*, his last film, but now he was very ill, in Paris. The arrival of his son, his mother-in-law, the Russians had held them hostage for seven years after Tarkovsky left Russia.

Scenes from his films. Strong, eerie images, the ability to create cinematic states that are beyond the visual, inner states in which one's understanding of things sharpens. Metaphysical fears, fears for the world, for those close to us, our desire to save them.

And then *Rublev*, that I saw many years ago and has remained in me as a magnificent achievement. The construction of the gigantic church bell by the young adolescent boy, trying to survive among plagues, killings, fears of reprisals, materials that he yet did not know how to find, how to handle.

A construction that involved an army of men, and finally the fear that it would not ring, have no resonance. When it does, the enthusiasm of the people, but he and the monk, Rublev, are left penniless on the empty road and have to take the hazardous journey again.

"Such a relief," she said, "to be able to talk to someone." She was talking to herself a lot, of course, then told herself to stop it. About her daughter who was coming to visit. Who got married again after her first husband died. They sent her a photo of the wedding. "They seemed," she said, "lyrically happy." We laughed. I said, how lovely, so very few people were lyrically happy nowadays.

"But how long will it last?" she asked.

A documentary on Isamu Noguchi, he was speaking of form, of materials, of stone specifically, as a human, living thing, sacred in its relationship to the universe, the oldness of stone, when we discover other planets the only thing we find are stones.

He had worked with Brancusi for six months in the thirties. How one must finally betray all one's teachers if one is to find oneself. How useful imaginative mistakes are, they show one directions one might not have taken.

The project that he was working on was the fountain and the gardens in the middle of Detroit, a marvelous thing. The fountain, as if a large knot, bringing forth water, light, fire, on the most magnificent scale.

DECEMBER

At the dinner, the Greek academic, a very young man doing his thesis on Cavafy, already looking old, carrying too much baggage, but quite vulnerable-looking, he seemed to approach poetry on tiptoe, afraid its bloom will disappear with rough handling.

Reading the new book. Enormous amount of work going on, theoretically, yet the intellect somehow turning on itself, as if in a tight circle out of which it is impossible to break out.

Or maybe it is my impression, they are turning round and round in it, getting dizzy, breathing in the fumes of escape, but the form itself as if a steel grid.

Some of Erik Satie's sayings: "Those who practice an art must live in a state of complete renunciation."

On his deathbed to a young musician: "One must remain intransigent up to the end."

And in his witty, comic writings: "Although our information is inaccurate, we do not guarantee it."

One could use this now with great accuracy about a lot of public statements.

From P. N. Furbank's biography of Diderot:

"Friendship, for him, was of supreme importance and an imperative duty for mankind: and in his *Letter On the Deaf and Dumb* he praises the law of the ancient Scythians which required all citizens to have at least a friend, allowed them to have two and forbade them three. He liked to surround all his activities with friendship. Thus his philosophical works tend to take the form of *Letters*."

In his *Salon* review of 1767, discussing a landscape by Vernet, he makes gentle fun of his own propensity:

"It is on behalf of myself and my friends that I read, that I reflect, that I write, meditate, listen, look and feel. In their absence, my devotion refers everything to them. I dream unceasingly of their happiness . . . It is to them that I have consecrated the use of all my senses and of all my faculties; and that is perhaps the reason why, in my imagination and talk, everything gets slightly improved and exaggerated. They sometimes reproach me for this, the ungrateful wretches."

ANTIGONE KEFALA (1931–2022) was born into a family of musicians in Brăila, Romania, and aspired to be an actor. Following the occupation by the Soviet Union, her family fled Romania, first escaping to Greece and living in refugee camps there. She spoke Romanian, French, Greek, and English, and completed an MA in French in New Zealand after arriving there as an adolescent. Kefala settled in Australia in 1959 and lived in Sydney until her death. She was the author of numerous works of fiction, including *The First Journey*, *The Island*, and *Alexia*, and five poetry collections, *The Alien*, *Thirsty Weather*, *European Notebook*, *Absence: New and Selected Poems*, and *Fragments*, which won the 2017 Judith Wright Calanthe Award and was shortlisted for the Prime Minister's Literary Award for Poetry. Her collections of journals—for which she received critical acclaim—include *Sydney Journals* and *Late Journals*, her final work. She was the recipient of the 2022 Patrick White Literary Award.

Transit Books is a nonprofit publisher of international and American literature, based in the San Francisco Bay Area. Founded in 2015, Transit Books is committed to the discovery and promotion of enduring works that carry readers across borders and communities. Visit us online to learn more about our forthcoming titles, events, and opportunities to support our mission.

TRANSITBOOKS.ORG